THE BEST OF relish
COOKBOOK

THE BEST OF relish COOKBOOK

celebrating America's love of food

FROM THE EDITORS OF *Relish* MAGAZINE

Jill Melton   Candace Floyd   Nancy S. Hughes

The Countryman Press

WOODSTOCK, VERMONT

LIBRARY OF CONGRESS CATALOGING-IN-PUBLICATION DATA

ISBN 978-0-88150-836-9

Photographs: Mark Boughton Photography; Teresa Blackburn, stylist, High Cotton Food Styling & Photography

Book design and composition by Vertigo Design

Published by The Countryman Press, P.O. Box 748, Woodstock, VT 05091

Distributed by W. W. Norton & Company, Inc., 500 Fifth Avenue, New York, NY 10110

10 9 8 7 6 5 4 3 2

acknowledgments

Without the help of many people, *The Best of Relish* would not have been possible.

Our thanks go to *Relish* magazine's executive editor, Charlie Cox, and director of business development, Steve Minucci, who cleared the way for this book's creation. Also to Publishing Group of America's president and CEO, Dick Porter.

Thanks also to Jean Kressy, who not only developed many of the recipes included in this book but also scrutinized, pondered and selected the 150 recipes printed here from our cache of more than 800.

For help in testing the recipes, our thanks go to Mary Carter, test kitchen director, who spent hours on end shopping, cooking and editing recipes.

For creating the beautiful photographs, thanks go to Mark Boughton, photographer; Teresa Blackburn, food stylist; Liz Shenk, assistant food stylist; and Karry Hosford of High Cotton Food Styling and Photography.

We're also grateful to Alison Lew of Vertigo, book designer; Elizabeth Parson, indexer; and Lisa Sacks, our editor at Countryman Press, who offered invaluable advice and expertise that was much appreciated.

introduction

EAT UP

It's hard to put together a book composed of your "bests" because along the way new bests keep presenting themselves. Thank heavens for publishers and deadlines because, left to our own devices, we would still be adding recipes to the book.

Speaking of bests, I consider *Relish* my own *personal* best. Launched in February 2006, it was the first food magazine to be distributed in newspapers nationally. Fast-forward three years to 2009, and *Relish* is in more than 500 newspapers and reaches 15 million readers. That's 15 million folks we get to educate, entertain and get excited about food.

People love to eat, but they love to talk about eating even more. I'm sure that you, just like me, have found yourself in the midst of lunch, talking about dinner. Everyone has a food story—whether it's a special cake you make for your child's birthday or a traditional Sunday family supper or a special pasta dish you concocted. And that's what *Relish* is about: celebrating and sharing food memories as well as creating new ones. We spotlight ordinary folks with extraordinary food stories—your neighbor's applesauce cookies, a Boston chef's roast chicken, a 92-year-old gardener and her homegrown tomatoes. We celebrate folks who are making an impact on what and how we eat: the goat farmer and cheesemaker in Vermont, the olive oil maker in California. We applaud those making a difference, like the advocate improving school lunches, the chef teaching kids about healthy cooking, the volunteer feeding the homeless. In addition, we report on new foods you'll find in your supermarket and new ways to cook old ones.

Our goal and hope is that the recipes in this book, a compilation of our best, will inspire you to head to the kitchen. Memories and traditions are created from cooking, sharing and eating together. Good things happen around the table.

Do you have a personal best food story? If so, we want to hear about it. Send your recipe and story to editorial@relishmag.com.

If you receive *Relish* in your local newspaper, bravo! If not, you can experience America's most widely read food magazine online at www.relishmag.com.

A friend of mine always says, "Good food matters." Indeed, it does.

JILL MELTON
Editor, *Relish*

Maple granola with cranberries and almonds

breakfasts

orange creamsicle smoothie

This smoothie tastes like a Creamsicle in a glass. Kids use their fine motor skills, practice math and learn how to safely operate kitchen equipment when they make this nutritious breakfast or snack drink. SERVES 2

1 cup fat-free milk

1 (6-ounce) container low-fat vanilla yogurt

⅓ cup calcium-fortified frozen orange juice concentrate

¼ teaspoon vanilla extract

5 ice cubes

Place all ingredients except ice cubes in a blender; process 15 seconds to combine. Add ice cubes and process 20 seconds to crush ice; serve immediately.

PER SERVING: Calories 180; fat 1.5g; chol. 5mg; prot. 9g; carbs. 32g; fiber 1g; sodium 135mg

maple granola with cranberries and almonds

To make this easy recipe even easier, measure the oil, swirl it around to coat the measuring cup, and add it to the saucepan. Then measure the syrup in the same cup. It will pour out without sticking to the sides. **SERVES 10**

4 cups old-fashioned oats

½ cup sliced almonds (about 2 ounces)

⅓ cup canola oil

½ cup maple syrup

¼ teaspoon ground cinnamon

Cooking spray

⅔ cup dried cranberries

1. Preheat oven to 325F.

2. Combine oats and almonds in a large bowl. Place oil, maple syrup and cinnamon in a small saucepan; bring to a boil over medium heat. Pour oil mixture over oat mixture; stir to combine. Spread oat mixture evenly in a roasting pan coated with cooking spray.

3. Bake 30 minutes or until golden brown, stirring occasionally. Cool in pan on a wire rack. Stir in cranberries.

PER SERVING: Calories 280; fat 13g; chol. 0mg; prot. 5g; carbs. 40g; fiber 4g; sodium 2mg

oven-poached eggs in spinach nests

For an easy Passover variation, substitute ½ cup matzo meal for flour in the spinach nests and substitute brown rice, cooked barley or potato pancakes for the English muffins. SERVES 8

SPINACH NESTS:

Cooking spray

3 eggs

½ cup all-purpose flour

1 pound small-curd cottage cheese

4 (10-ounce) packages frozen chopped spinach, thawed, drained and squeezed dry

½ teaspoon salt

Coarsely ground black pepper

EGGS:

8 eggs

1 cup (4 ounces) shredded Swiss or grated Parmigiano-Reggiano cheese

4 English muffins, split and toasted

½ cup thinly sliced red bell pepper (optional)

½ cup vertically sliced onion (optional)

1. Preheat oven to 350F. Coat a 13 x 9-inch baking dish with cooking spray.

2. To prepare spinach nests, combine eggs, flour and cottage cheese; whisk well. Add spinach, salt and pepper; stir well to combine. (This can be done up to 2 days ahead).

3. Press mixture into prepared dish. Make 8 indentations with the back of a spoon (this is where the eggs will be placed). Bake 25 minutes.

4. Remove pan from oven and, using a spoon, hollow the nests out deeper. Break an egg into each indentation. Bake 15 minutes or until whites are set. Sprinkle with cheese; bake an additional 1 minute.

5. Place 1 egg and spinach nest on each English muffin half. Garnish with red pepper and onion, if desired.

PER SERVING: Calories 330; fat 14g; chol. 315mg; prot. 24g; carbs. 24g; fiber 3g; sodium 720mg

huevos rancheros

Spanish for "rancher's eggs," Huevos Rancheros consists of fried eggs on corn tortillas topped with salsa. SERVES 4

5 teaspoons vegetable oil, divided

¼ cup chopped onion

1 small jalapeno pepper, seeded and minced

1 (14½-ounce) can diced tomatoes

½ teaspoon sugar

⅛ teaspoon salt

⅛ teaspoon black pepper

4 corn tortillas

1 tablespoon butter

4 large eggs

½ cup (2 ounces) shredded Monterey Jack cheese

Chopped fresh cilantro

1. Heat 3 teaspoons oil in a medium saucepan over medium heat. Add onion and pepper; cook until onion is soft and starting to brown, about 3 minutes, stirring occasionally. Add tomatoes, sugar, salt and pepper. Simmer, stirring occasionally, until sauce is slightly thickened, about 10 minutes. Cover; keep warm over very low heat.

2. Preheat oven to 200F.

3. Brush tortillas on both sides with 2 teaspoons oil. Heat a medium skillet over medium-high heat until hot. Add tortillas one at a time; cook until golden brown in spots, 30 to 60 seconds on each side. Wrap in foil and place in oven to keep warm.

4. Melt butter in a large nonstick skillet over medium-low heat. Add eggs and fry until whites are partially set, about 1 minute. Cover and cook until eggs are set, 3 to 4 minutes. Place a tortilla on each of 4 warmed plates. Top each tortilla with a fried egg and sauce; sprinkle with cheese and cilantro.

PER SERVING: Calories 300; fat 19g; chol. 230mg; prot. 12g; carbs. 19g; fiber 2g; sodium 510mg

spanish tortilla

Not to be confused with Mexican tortillas, this Spanish dish is actually an omelet made with eggs, onions and potatoes. Serve with prepared salsa.   SERVES 4

4 eggs

½ teaspoon kosher salt

Coarsely ground black pepper

2 tablespoons olive oil, divided

1 small peeled baking potato, thinly sliced

½ small yellow onion, thinly sliced

1. Place eggs, salt and pepper in a large bowl; beat to combine.

2. Heat 1 tablespoon oil in a medium nonstick skillet over medium heat. Add potato and cook until soft, about 5 minutes.

3. Add onion to pan; cook 5 minutes, stirring occasionally. Add to egg mixture; stir to mix well.

4. Place 1 tablespoon oil in pan; heat over medium heat. Pour in egg mixture and cook until omelet begins to set, 7 to 8 minutes. Carefully flip to cook other side. (To flip omelet, slide onto a plate, place skillet over plate and invert.) Cook 2 to 3 minutes. Cut into wedges. Serve hot, room temperature or cold.

PER SERVING: Calories 180; fat 12g; chol. 210mg; prot. 7g; carbs. 10g; fiber 1g; sodium 310mg

red pepper, egg and provolone panini

In the south of Italy, egg and bell pepper sandwiches are a classic. For variety, add sautéed or grilled red onion slices. **SERVES 2**

3 eggs

¾ teaspoon dried oregano

¼ teaspoon salt

¼ teaspoon black pepper

½ cup bottled roasted red bell peppers, drained

2 ounces sliced sharp Provolone cheese

1 ounce Parmigiano-Reggiano cheese, sliced

4 slices (½-inch-thick) Sicilian-style sesame semolina bread

Olive oil

1. Preheat panini grill or stovetop griddle pan.

2. Place eggs, oregano, salt and pepper in a small bowl; beat with a fork. Heat a nonstick skillet over medium-high heat; add egg mixture and cook until set, 2 to 3 minutes, occasionally lifting edges with a fork to allow uncooked eggs to run underneath.

3. Divide cooked eggs, pepper and cheeses between 2 slices bread. Top with remaining bread. Brush outsides lightly with olive oil.

4. Place on panini grill or griddle; cover with grill top or grill press. Grill 2 to 3 minutes on each side, until golden and cheese starts to melt.

PER SERVING: Calories 420; fat 22g; chol. 345mg; prot. 26g; carbs. 27g; fiber 1g; sodium 1210mg

pumpkin cheddar muffins

These savory muffins are studded with poblano peppers and Cheddar cheese, making them a perfect accompaniment to soup or chili. SERVES 12

STREUSEL TOPPING:

3 tablespoons all-purpose flour

1 tablespoon butter

⅓ cup finely shredded extra-sharp Cheddar cheese

1 tablespoon brown sugar

⅛ teaspoon cayenne

⅓ cup roasted salted pepitas (pumpkin seeds)

MUFFINS:

1 cup all-purpose flour

¾ cup stone-ground yellow cornmeal

¼ teaspoon salt

2½ teaspoons baking powder

½ teaspoon baking soda

1 egg

¾ cup buttermilk

¼ cup packed dark brown sugar

3 tablespoons butter, melted

¾ cup canned pumpkin

2 roasted poblano peppers, peeled, seeded and finely diced, or ¼ cup chopped canned green chiles

Cooking spray

1. Preheat oven to 400F.

2. To prepare streusel, combine flour and butter with a pastry blender or 2 knives until crumbly. Add cheese, brown sugar and cayenne. Stir in pepitas.

3. To prepare muffins, combine flour and next 4 ingredients (flour through baking soda) in a large bowl; set aside. Combine egg and next 4 ingredients (egg through pumpkin) in a medium bowl; whisk to combine thoroughly. Stir egg mixture into flour mixture. Gently stir in poblano peppers. Spoon batter into muffin cups coated with cooking spray; sprinkle streusel topping over each muffin.

4. Bake 15 to 20 minutes, until golden brown.

PER SERVING: Calories 190; fat 9g; chol. 30mg; prot. 6g; carbs. 24g; fiber 2g; sodium 300mg

---

to measure flour, *lightly spoon it into a measuring cup and level it off with a knife.*

refrigerator bran muffins

Make the batter in advance, ladle into a sealable plastic container, and refrigerate up to two weeks. This is a great base for all sorts of add-ins. Try shredded carrot, raisins, dried cranberries or pineapple. **MAKES 24 MUFFINS**

2 cups All-Bran cereal

⅔ cup wheat bran

1⅓ cups boiling water

2⅔ cups all-purpose flour

1 tablespoon baking soda

1 teaspoon ground cinnamon

½ teaspoon salt

¼ teaspoon grated or ground nutmeg

Cooking spray

2 cups buttermilk

½ cup pasteurized egg substitute or 2 eggs

1 cup granulated sugar

½ cup firmly packed light brown sugar

½ cup vegetable oil

1 teaspoon vanilla extract

1. Mix cereal and wheat bran in a large bowl. Add boiling water, stir well and set aside 1 hour.

2. Whisk together flour, baking soda, cinnamon, salt and nutmeg in a medium bowl.

3. Preheat oven to 375F. Coat muffin cups with cooking spray.

4. Add 1 cup buttermilk to bran mixture; stir well with a whisk. Add remaining buttermilk, egg substitute, granulated sugar, brown sugar, oil and vanilla, stirring until smooth.

5. Add flour mixture; stir until a thick batter forms.

6. Fill each cup with ⅔ cup muffin batter. Bake 20 to 25 minutes, until puffed and lightly browned.

PER SERVING: Calories 150; fat 5g; chol. 0mg; prot. 3g; carbs. 26g; fiber 2g fiber; sodium 250mg

apple puff-up pancake

Kids love watching this eggy batter puff in the oven like magic. We've added apples to this pancake, known as a Dutch Baby or German Pancake, for added flavor and nutrition.   SERVES 4

½ cup all-purpose flour

½ cup whole milk

3 eggs, room temperature

¼ teaspoon vanilla extract

2 tablespoons butter

1 large peeled, sliced, Granny Smith apple

¼ cup packed dark brown sugar

¼ teaspoon ground cinnamon

Fresh lemon juice

Powdered sugar

1. Preheat oven to 450F.

2. Place flour, milk, eggs and vanilla in a medium bowl; beat with a whisk until smooth.

3. Melt butter in a 10-inch cast iron or other ovenproof skillet over medium heat. Place apples in pan and cook 4 minutes. Turn apples and cook an additional 3 minutes. Sprinkle brown sugar and cinnamon over apples and cook until sugar begins to melt, about 1 minute; remove pan from heat. Stir apples lightly to coat with sugar. Spread evenly in pan; pour batter over apples.

4. Place on center rack in oven and bake 15 minutes or until mixture puffs and turns golden brown around edges. Remove from oven. Cut into four wedges. Sprinkle with lemon juice and powdered sugar. Serve warm.

PER SERVING: Calories 240; fat 10g; chol. 175mg; prot. 7g; carbs. 31g; fiber 1g; sodium 65mg

date nut brown bread

Here's a take on Boston Brown Bread: baked, not steamed, but with molasses and cornmeal like the original. The dates offer plenty of richness without additional fat. SERVES 12

2 cups finely chopped pitted dates (about 10 ounces)

6 tablespoons butter

1 cup 2% reduced-fat milk

¼ cup unsulfured molasses

Cooking spray

1⅔ cups all-purpose flour

⅔ cup yellow cornmeal

1 teaspoon baking powder

½ teaspoon baking soda

½ teaspoon salt

½ teaspoon ground cinnamon

1 egg, room temperature

⅔ cup sugar

½ teaspoon vanilla extract

1 cup toasted pecan halves, chopped

1. Place first 4 ingredients in a medium saucepan over medium heat. Stir until butter melts and mixture begins to simmer; remove from heat. Transfer to a large bowl; cool to room temperature.

2. Preheat oven to 325F. Coat a 9 x 5-inch loaf pan with cooking spray; dust with flour.

3. Combine flour and next 5 ingredients (flour through cinnamon) in a medium bowl; set aside.

4. Place egg, sugar and vanilla in a medium bowl; whisk until well blended. Add egg mixture to cooled date mixture; stir well. Add pecans and flour mixture to date mixture; stir until well blended. Spoon mixture into prepared pan; spread evenly.

5. Bake 1 hour and 10 minutes or until wooden pick inserted in the center comes out clean. Cool 10 minutes in pan on a wire rack. Remove from pan. Cool completely on wire rack.

NOTE: To make the bread in cans, double the recipe and bake in 3 (4½ cup-capacity) cans for about 1 hour.

PER SERVING: Calories 330; fat 13g; chol. 35mg; prot. 5g; carbs. 54g; fiber 4g; sodium 210mg

banana breakfast coffee cake

A brown sugar streusel with chopped walnuts adds richness and crunch to this tender banana cake. SERVES 10

TOPPING:

½ cup all-purpose flour

½ cup packed light brown sugar

1 teaspoon ground cinnamon

6 tablespoons unsalted butter, chilled

½ cup finely chopped walnuts

CAKE:

2 cups all-purpose flour

1 teaspoon baking soda

1 teaspoon baking powder

½ teaspoon ground nutmeg

½ teaspoon salt

½ cup unsalted butter, softened

⅔ cup granulated sugar

2 eggs

1 cup mashed very ripe bananas

1 teaspoon vanilla extract

⅓ cup 2% reduced-fat milk

Cooking spray

1. Preheat oven to 350F.

2. To prepare topping, combine flour, brown sugar, cinnamon and butter in a food processor; process until mixture resembles fine crumbs. Stir in walnuts; set aside.

3. To prepare cake, combine flour and next 4 ingredients (flour through salt) in a medium bowl; set aside.

4. Place butter in a large bowl; beat with a mixer at medium speed until smooth, about 30 seconds. Gradually add sugar; beat until fluffy, 3 to 4 minutes. Add eggs, 1 at a time, beating well after each addition. Add bananas and vanilla; beat until well blended. Add flour mixture and milk alternately to sugar mixture, mixing after each addition only until smooth. Pour batter into a 9-inch square baking ban coated with cooking spray; sprinkle with topping.

5. Bake about 35 minutes, until wooden pick inserted in the center comes out clean. Cool in pan on a wire rack. Serve warm or at room temperature.

PER SERVING: Calories 370; fat 20g; chol. 45mg; prot. 4g; carbs. 48g; fiber 1g; sodium 300mg.

oatmeal breakfast cake

For those with a sweet tooth, here's a coffeecake that incorporates oatmeal. While not as high in fiber as a bowl of oatmeal, it's a tasty way to get some of its benefits. SERVES 16

Cooking spray

1 cup all-purpose flour

1 cup old-fashioned oats

1 cup graham cracker crumbs

¾ cup packed brown sugar

⅓ cup granulated sugar

1 teaspoon baking powder

1 teaspoon baking soda

½ teaspoon ground cinnamon

½ teaspoon salt

½ cup vegetable oil

1 cup buttermilk

3 eggs

1. Preheat oven to 350F. Coat a 12-cup bundt pan with cooking spray.

2. Combine flour and next 8 ingredients (flour through salt) in a large bowl. Place oil, buttermilk and eggs in a medium bowl; whisk to combine. Add buttermilk mixture to flour mixture; whisk to combine.

3. Spoon batter into prepared pan. Bake 40 minutes or until wooden pick inserted in the center comes out clean. Cool on a wire rack 10 minutes. Remove from pan; cool completely on wire rack.

PER SERVING: Calories 190; fat 9g; chol. 40mg; prot. 4g; carbs. 26g; fiber 1g; sodium 130mg

don't have the buttermilk the cake recipe calls for?
No worries. In baked goods, you can substitute an equal amount of yogurt or light sour cream.

cherry cream cheese coffee cake

Have your cake and streusel, too—for breakfast. SERVES 9

STREUSEL:

¼ cup all-purpose flour

2 tablespoons granulated sugar

2 tablespoons light brown sugar

2 tablespoons cold butter, cut into small pieces

3 tablespoons sliced almonds

FILLING:

½ cup (4 ounces) block-style ⅓-less-fat cream cheese, softened

3 tablespoons granulated sugar

CAKE:

1¼ cups all-purpose flour

1 teaspoon baking powder

¼ teaspoon salt

6 tablespoons unsalted butter

⅔ cup granulated sugar

1 egg

¾ teaspoon vanilla extract

¼ teaspoon almond extract

⅔ cup 2% reduced-fat milk

Cooking spray

2 cups pitted cherries (about 10 ounces)

1. Preheat oven to 350F.

2. To prepare streusel, combine flour and sugars in a medium bowl. Cut in butter with a pastry blender or two knives until crumbly. Stir in almonds; set aside.

3. To prepare filling, combine cream cheese and granulated sugar; stir just until smooth.

4. To prepare cake, combine flour, baking powder and salt in a medium bowl; set aside. Place butter and next 4 ingredients (butter through almond extract) in large bowl; beat with mixer on medium speed until evenly blended. Add flour mixture and milk alternately to sugar mixture, beginning and ending with flour mixture; beat at low speed until blended. Pour into a 9-inch square baking pan coated with cooking spray; top with small spoonfuls of filling. Spoon cherries over filling and sprinkle with streusel mixture.

5. Bake 50 minutes or until cake begins to pull away from sides of pan. Cool in pan on wire rack; serve warm.

PER SERVING: Calories 290; fat 13g; chol. 55mg; prot. 5g; carbs. 41g; fiber 2g; sodium 200mg

mandarin punch

new mexican tomatillo salsa

toasted walnut and sun-dried tomato dip

spinach pesto

classic pimiento cheese

meatballs in sofrito sauce

lime refresher

melon rum punch

prosecco sunrise punch

mandarin punch

watermelon-mint ice cubes

appetizers & beverages

new mexican tomatillo salsa

Take a break from the typical tomato-based salsa. Serve this green salsa with chips, fish or cheese quesadillas. SERVES 7

3 fresh tomatillos

2 Anaheim chile peppers, seeded and chopped

2 tablespoons chopped fresh parsley

2 shallots, minced, or ½ small white onion, minced

1 garlic clove, minced

2 tablespoons lime juice

½ teaspoon salt

1. Discard husks and stems from tomatillos and finely chop.

2. Combine all ingredients in a bowl. Serve immediately or cover and chill up to 12 hours.

PER SERVING: Calories 20; fat 0g; chol. 0mg; prot. 1g; carbs. 5g; fiber 0g; sodium 170mg

toasted walnut and sun-dried tomato dip

You'll want to have this versatile dip on hand all summer. Traditionally, it's served with pita chips, baby carrots or thickly sliced cucumber rounds, but try it as a sandwich spread or tossed with warm pasta, too. SERVES 8

2 cups boiling water

3 ounces sun-dried tomatoes, packed without oil (about 36)

1½ cups walnuts, toasted

¾ cup chopped bottled roasted red bell peppers

1 garlic clove, peeled

2 teaspoons balsamic vinegar

½ teaspoon fennel seeds

½ teaspoon salt

½ teaspoon black pepper

¼ teaspoon ground cinnamon

1. Combine 2 cups boiling water and sun-dried tomatoes in a bowl; let stand 1 hour or until soft. Drain tomatoes over a bowl, reserving ½ cup liquid.

2. Place tomatoes, ½ cup liquid and remaining ingredients in a food processor; pulse a few times, then process until well blended.

3. Spoon into a medium bowl. Cover and refrigerate up to 3 days. Serve at room temperature.

PER SERVING: Calories 180; fat 15g; chol. 0mg; prot. 5g; carbs. 11g; fiber 4g; sodium 440mg

spinach pesto

Use this pesto in pasta salads, on grilled chicken breasts or on bruschetta. It will keep in the refrigerator for several days.   SERVES 20

1 (9-ounce) bag fresh spinach (about 8 cups), trimmed, divided

1 cup packed basil leaves

½ cup pine nuts, toasted

1 garlic clove, peeled

⅔ cup extra-virgin olive oil

⅔ cup grated Parmigiano-Reggiano cheese

½ teaspoon salt

Coarsely ground black pepper

1.   Place half of spinach, basil, pine nuts and garlic in a food processor; process until finely chopped. Add remaining spinach; process until smooth. With processor on, slowly pour oil through food chute; process until well blended.

2.   Spoon into a bowl. Stir in remaining ingredients. Store in refrigerator.

PER SERVING: Calories 110; fat 11g; chol. omg; prot. 2g; carbs. 2g; fiber 1g; sodium 120mg

classic pimiento cheese

If you've never had homemade pimiento cheese, you're in for a treat. SERVES 5

2 cups (8 ounces) finely shredded extra-sharp Cheddar cheese, divided

½ cup (2 ounces) finely grated Parmigiano-Reggiano cheese, divided

⅓ cup mayonnaise, divided

1 (4-ounce) jar diced pimientos, drained (reserving 1 tablespoon liquid)

1 tablespoon minced shallot or yellow onion

1 small garlic clove, crushed

Dash of ground red pepper

Dash of dry mustard

1. Combine half of Cheddar and Parmesan cheese and ¼ cup mayonnaise; stir until well blended. Add remaining cheese, pimiento and reserved liquid, shallot, garlic, pepper and dry mustard. Cover and refrigerate 30 minutes.

2. For a thinner consistency, add remaining mayonnaise.

PER SERVING: Calories 320; fat 11g; chol. 60mg; prot. 15g; carbs. 3g; fiber 0g; sodium 510 mg

meatballs in sofrito sauce

Sofrito is a rich sautéed mixture of onions, peppers and garlic that makes for a great tomato sauce. It is used in many Puerto Rican dishes. Use a lean ground beef, but not the leanest, so that the meatballs will be tender. SERVES 10

SOFRITO SAUCE:

2 tablespoons vegetable oil

1 cup chopped onion

1 cup chopped red or green bell pepper

2 garlic cloves, minced

1 (14½-ounce) can diced tomatoes, undrained

½ cup water

⅓ cup cilantro sprigs

½ teaspoon salt

Coarsely ground black pepper

MEATBALLS:

1 pound lean ground beef

⅓ cup chopped pimiento-stuffed green olives

1 egg, lightly beaten

3 tablespoons dried breadcrumbs

2 large garlic cloves, minced

½ teaspoon dried oregano

½ teaspoon salt

Coarsely ground black pepper

2 tablespoons vegetable oil

LIME-CILANTRO GREMOLATA:

1 medium lime

1 tablespoon minced fresh cilantro

2 large garlic cloves, minced

1. To prepare Sofrito Sauce, heat oil in a medium saucepan over medium high heat. Add onion, bell pepper and garlic; sauté 10 minutes or until tender.

2. Place onion mixture and remaining ingredients in blender or food processor; process until smooth. Set aside.

3. To prepare meatballs, combine beef and next 7 ingredients (beef through pepper) in a medium bowl; shape mixture into 30 (1-inch) meatballs. Heat oil in a large nonstick skillet over medium heat. Add meatballs; cook until brown on all sides, about 6 minutes. Drain well; return to pan.

4. Add reserved sofrito sauce; bring to boil. Cover, reduce heat, and simmer 10 minutes. Uncover and cook until meatballs are done and sauce thickens, about 5 minutes, stirring occasionally. Spoon into a serving bowl or individual shot glasses.

5. To prepare Gremolata, grate rind from lime, reserving lime for another use. Combine lime rind, cilantro and garlic in a small bowl. Sprinkle over meatballs.

PER SERVING: Calories 120; fat 8g; chol. 40mg; prot. 8g; carbs. 5g; fiber 1g; sodium 410mg

lime refresher

Every party needs a colorful nonalcoholic drink that makes non-imbibers feel included in the fun. Inspired by the Bacardi Cocktail (a daiquiri with grenadine), this one has all the refreshment of that classic drink—without the rum. SERVES 1

2 tablespoons lime juice

2 teaspoons grenadine

1 teaspoon sugar

¼ teaspoon vanilla extract

Ice cubes

½ cup club soda

Mint leaves (optional)

1. Combine lime juice, grenadine, sugar and vanilla in a tall glass. Stir to partially dissolve sugar.

2. Fill glass with ice; pour in club soda and stir. Garnish with mint, if desired. Serve immediately.

PER SERVING: Calories 60; fat 0g; chol. 0mg; prot. 0g; carbs. 15g; fiber 0g; sodium 30mg

melon rum punch

Flavored rums have hit the market in recent years, making island-style rum punches better than ever. This one contrasts fresh tropical-fruit flavors with zippy citrus and bitters for pure refreshment—with a kick, of course. SERVES 8

3 cups guava or mango nectar

3 cups pineapple juice

1½ cups melon-flavored rum

¼ cup grenadine

¾ cup lime juice (about 6 medium limes)

2 teaspoons angostura bitters

1 cup orange or lime slices

1 cup watermelon chunks or balls

1 cup maraschino cherries

1. Combine first 6 ingredients in a large pitcher; chill.

2. Stir in orange slices, watermelon and cherries. Pour over ice.

PER SERVING: Calories 250; fat 0g; chol. 0mg; prot. 0g; carbs. 39g; fiber 1g; sodium 10mg

prosecco sunrise punch

What better way to start a holiday brunch than with this very grown-up, easy-to-drink sparkling punch. We love the beautiful color—orange tinged with red—which seems to make the
table come alive. Just think, all that and vitamin C, too. SERVES 12

1 (750ml) bottle sparkling wine,
such as prosecco, chilled

3¼ cups orange juice, chilled

2 cups orange-flavored
seltzer, chilled

½ cup orange-flavored
liqueur, such as triple sec

¼ cup grenadine

6 orange slices, halved

1.   Combine sparkling wine, orange juice, seltzer and liqueur in a bowl.
Ladle into 12 champagne flutes or wine glasses.

2.   Slowly pour 1 teaspoon of grenadine into each. Garnish rim of glasses
with half an orange slice. Serve immediately.

PER SERVING: Calories 130; fat 0g; chol. 0mg; prot. 0g; carbs. 22g; fiber 0g;
sodium 10mg

mandarin punch

Put a little more "punch" in this punch by adding a splash of ginger ale right before serving.

1 large ripe banana

1¼ cups pineapple juice

1 quart fresh satsuma,
tangerine or orange juice

1 cup gold rum

½ cup orange-flavored
liqueur, such as Cointreau

¼ cup dark rum, such as Myers

¼ cup lime juice

2 tablespoons grenadine

¼ teaspoon salt

Combine banana and pineapple juice in a blender or food processor;
process until smooth. Pour into large pitcher. Stir in remaining ingredients.
Pour over ice. SERVES 8

PER SERVING: Calories 250; fat 0g; chol. 0mg; prot. 0g; carbs. 35g; fiber 0g;
sodium 110mg

watermelon-mint ice cubes

Your kids will love these after a long, hot day outdoors. Serve with water or lemonade.

1½ cups cubed seeded watermelon

½ cup water

1 tablespoon sugar

2 tablespoons lemon juice

1 tablespoon honey

24 small mint leaves

1. Place watermelon, water, sugar, lemon juice and honey in a blender or food processor; process until smooth.

2. Place mint leaves in ice cube trays. Pour watermelon mixture over mint leaves; freeze 4 hours or until firm.

PER SERVING: Calories 20; fat 0g; chol. 0mg; prot. 0g; carbs. 6g; fiber 0g; sodium 0mg

variation: *To make watermelon granita, pour mixture in a 9-inch square pan. Stir in chopped mint and freeze. Scrape with a fork to form ice crystals.*

saimin

soups

minestrone

With canned tomatoes and canned beans, this vegetable soup comes together quickly. SERVES 6

2 tablespoons olive oil

1 cup diced onion (about 1 medium)

1 cup diced carrots (about 2 medium)

¾ cup diced celery (about 3 stalks)

2 medium zucchini, diced

1 garlic clove, minced

3 diced unpeeled medium potatoes (about ¾ pound)

3 cups thinly sliced Savoy cabbage

1 (15½-ounce) can cannellini beans, rinsed and drained

1 (14½-ounce) can diced tomatoes, undrained

2 (14-ounce) cans low-sodium chicken broth

3 cups water

½ teaspoon crushed dried rosemary

½ teaspoon salt

½ teaspoon coarsely ground black pepper

Grated Parmigiano-Reggiano cheese (optional)

Heat oil in a large saucepan over medium heat. Add onion; cook until softened, stirring occasionally, about 6 minutes. Add carrots and celery; cook 3 minutes, stirring occasionally. Add zucchini and garlic; cook 3 minutes, stirring occasionally. Add potatoes and cabbage; continue cooking and stirring another 3 minutes. Add remaining ingredients except cheese. Cover and bring to a simmer. Simmer gently 1 to 2 hours. Serve with Parmesan cheese, if desired.

PER SERVING: Calories 200; fat 5g; chol. 5mg; prot. 7g; carbs. 31g; fiber 7g; sodium 900mg

dressed-up tomato soup

We all know it's accessories that count. Here, canned tomato soup is outfitted with cheese, sweet grape tomatoes and crispy bacon, taking it from simple to spectacular. It also adds a calcium boost of 600 milligrams—as much as is in 2 cups of milk. Serve with toasted bagels. **SERVES 2**

1 (10½ -ounce) can condensed tomato soup

1 can 2% reduced-fat milk

10 grape tomatoes, halved

2 bacon slices, cooked and crumbled

1 (1-ounce) mozzarella cheese stick, cut into 6 pieces

1 cup spinach, chopped

½ cup (2 ounces) finely grated Parmigiano-Reggiano cheese

Place soup in saucepan. Add milk; stir with whisk to combine. Add tomatoes. Bring to a boil, reduce heat and simmer 5 minutes. Remove from heat; add bacon, mozzarella cheese and spinach. Ladle into bowls and sprinkle with Parmigiano-Reggiano.

PER SERVING: Calories 360; fat 13g; chol. 40mg; prot. 21g; carbs. 38g; fiber 2g; sodium 1570mg

weeknight white bean soup with swiss chard

You can use spinach or any kind of green in place of the chard. **SERVES 8**

1 tablespoon olive oil

1 fennel bulb, chopped

3 leeks, thinly sliced
(white part only)

2 (15-ounce) cans cannellini
beans, rinsed and drained

¼ teaspoon coarsely
ground black pepper

6 cups low-sodium vegetable broth

1 bunch Swiss chard,
coarsely chopped

8 baguette slices

¾ cup shredded Gruyère cheese

1. Heat olive oil in a Dutch oven over medium-high heat. Add fennel and leeks; sauté 5 minutes. Add beans, pepper and broth. Bring to a simmer. If desired, mash some of beans with a potato masher to make a creamy consistency. Stir in Swiss chard; cook until tender, 10 to 15 minutes.

2. Preheat oven to 400F.

3. Top baguette slices with cheese. Toast in oven until cheese melts and bread is crispy. Serve with soup.

PER SERVING: Calories 220; fat 6g; chol. 10mg; prot. 10g; carbs. 32g; fiber 7g; sodium 540mg

wild mushroom, bean and barley soup mix

This mix makes six 1-pint jars or twelve 1-cup jars. Layered as described here, the mix is so pretty your friends may put off making the soup. MAKES 6 (1-PINT) OR 12 (1-CUP) JARS

1 tablespoon coarsely ground black pepper

1½ cups dried small red lentils

6 bay leaves

3 cups uncooked pearl barley

1½ cups dried porcini and shiitake mushrooms, cut into ½-inch pieces

1½ cups dried yellow split peas

¾ cup mixed dried vegetables for soup (such as Just Corn, Just Peas and Just Tomatoes)

2 tablespoons dried dill weed

1. Place ½ teaspoon black pepper in the bottom of 6 (1-pint) jars. (If making in 8-ounce jars, halve all ingredients.) Pour ¼ cup red lentils into each jar.

2. Place one bay leaf in each jar, vertically against the inside of the glass, anchoring the tip in the lentils. Pour ½ cup barley into each jar, holding bay leaf against jar until the barley keeps it in place.

3. Place ¼ cup mushrooms in each jar. Press down to eliminate air pockets.

4. Pour ¼ cup split peas in each jar, followed by 2 heaping tablespoons of dried vegetables and 1 teaspoon dill weed. Place lid on each jar and tighten.

wild mushroom, bean and barley soup SERVES 8

1 pint wild mushroom, bean and barley soup mix

4 cups water

4 cups vegetable broth, divided

1 teaspoon salt

1. Combine soup mix, water and 2 cups broth in a large saucepan over medium-high heat. Bring to a boil; stir well, reduce heat and simmer, covered, 45 minutes.

2. Add 2 cups broth and salt. Return to boil, reduce heat, and simmer until barley and peas are tender, 40 to 50 minutes, stirring occasionally.

PER SERVING: Calories 110; fat 0g; chol. 0mg; prot. 5g; carbs. 22g; fiber 4g; sodium 520mg

irish potato soup with cheese and red ale

You may use all leeks or all onions instead of a combination of the two; the potatoes may be peeled or unpeeled; and you may use a more readily available beer or ale. You can also use chicken stock instead of vegetable and add a garnish of crisp bacon crumbles. Serve with a spinach salad and whole grain toast or crisp baguette slices. SERVES 8

4 tablespoons butter, divided

2 tablespoons vegetable oil

2 cups chopped onion (about 2 medium)

2 leeks, sliced

¾ cup sliced celery (about 3 stalks)

8 medium Yukon Gold potatoes, cubed

1 (12-ounce) bottle Irish red ale

5 cups low-sodium chicken or vegetable broth

½ teaspoon salt

Coarsely ground black pepper

3 tablespoons all-purpose flour

4 cups whole or 2% reduced-fat milk

2 cups (8 ounces) shredded Kerrygold Dubliner cheese or 4 ounces Gruyère and 8 ounces sharp white Cheddar

GARNISHES:

¾ cup finely minced parsley (optional)

4 ounces crumbled blue cheese (optional)

Bacon slices, cooked and crumbled (optional)

1. Melt 2 tablespoons butter in a 6-quart stockpot. Add oil, onion, leeks and celery; stir. Cook over medium heat about 10 minutes; add potatoes, ale, broth, salt and pepper. Bring to a boil; simmer, covered, over low heat, until potatoes are tender, about 1 hour.

2. Melt 2 tablespoons butter in a medium saucepan. Gradually add flour, stirring with a whisk until smooth. Cook 3 minutes over medium-low heat, stirring constantly. Slowly add milk, stirring with a whisk until hot and thickened. Add cheese; stir until melted.

3. Slowly add sauce to potato mixture; stir well to combine. Cook over very low heat 10 minutes.

4. Ladle into soup bowls and sprinkle with parsley, blue cheese and bacon, if desired.

PER SERVING: Calories 480; fat 22g; chol. 60mg; prot. 17g; carbs. 51g; fiber 4g; sodium 740mg

gazpacho

At the top of the list of recipes we like to make when the weather gets really hot is gazpacho. This cold soup, from the Andalusia region of southern Spain, is a wonderful midsummer treat. Try serving Gazpacho in shot glasses at your next tapas party. **SERVES 6**

1 cup stale French bread cubes, crusts removed

Cold water

3 cups diced peeled tomatoes (about 1½ pounds)

⅔ cup diced green bell pepper

⅔ cup diced peeled English cucumber

⅓ cup diced red onion

2 garlic cloves, minced

1½ cups tomato juice

2 tablespoons extra-virgin olive oil

2 tablespoons red wine vinegar

½ teaspoon salt

Coarsely ground black pepper

Minced green bell pepper and cucumber (for garnish)

1. Place bread cubes in a small bowl and cover with water. Let stand 5 minutes or until bread is soft. Squeeze water from bread. Place bread, tomatoes and next 4 ingredients (bread through garlic) in a food processor; process to a coarse purée.

2. Pour mixture into a large bowl; add remaining ingredients except garnish. Cover; chill 4 hours or until cold. Ladle into bowls and garnish with minced bell pepper and cucumber.

PER SERVING: Calories 180; fat 6g; chol. 0mg; prot. 5g; carbs. 27g; fiber 3g; sodium 580mg

to peel tomatoes, *dunk them in boiling water for a minute. Then plunge in cold water. The peels will slip off.*

classic chicken soup with matzo balls

As good as 10 Jewish mothers.

SOUP:

1 (4- to 5-pound) chicken, giblets removed

2 celery stalks with leaves, halved

1 medium onion, quartered

3 carrots, peeled and halved

1 parsnip, peeled and halved

4 sprigs fresh flat-leaf parsley

4 sprigs fresh dill

1 tablespoon salt

½ teaspoon coarsely ground black pepper

MATZO BALLS:

2 eggs

2 tablespoons vegetable oil

1 teaspoon salt

2 tablespoons unflavored seltzer or club soda

½ cup unsalted matzo meal

1. To prepare soup, place chicken in an 8-quart Dutch oven or stockpot; add cold water to cover completely. Add remaining ingredients; bring to a boil. Reduce heat to low; cook, covered, 2 hours. Remove chicken from broth. Strain broth through a cheesecloth-lined colander into a bowl; discard solids. Reserve chicken for another use. Refrigerate broth several hours or overnight.

2. To prepare matzo balls, beat eggs in a large bowl with whisk until lemon-colored. Add oil, salt and seltzer; beat well. Mix in matzo meal; do not over mix. Let stand several minutes.

3. Bring water to a boil in a half-filled Dutch oven or stockpot. Form matzo mixture into 8 balls, using wet hands. Reduce heat to low and carefully place matzo balls into water. Cover pot; simmer 45 to 60 minutes. Matzo balls are done when white and fluffy in the center. If yellow, cook 10 more minutes.

4. To serve, scrape off the layer of fat from the top of broth; reheat. Add cooked matzo balls.

PER SERVING: Calories 100; fat 5g; chol. 60mg; prot. 4g; carbs. 8g; fiber 0g; sodium 1510mg

make a quick chicken stock *from the bones of a rotisserie chicken: Place chicken bones, an onion and enough water to cover them in a large saucepan. Bring to a boil, reduce heat and simmer 1 to 2 hours.*

weeknight chicken vegetable soup

Canned chicken broth is enhanced with garlic, onions, ginger and parsnips for a quick flavorful soup. Add rotisserie chicken, and dinner is done. **SERVES 10**

1 tablespoon olive oil

3 garlic cloves, chopped

2 medium onions, chopped

1 (2-inch) piece peeled fresh ginger, chopped

3 carrots, peeled and sliced

2 parsnips, peeled and sliced

9 cups low-sodium chicken broth

1½ teaspoons salt

½ teaspoon coarsely ground black pepper

1 (3-pound) rotisserie chicken, skinned and shredded

2 cups cooked egg noodles

1. Heat olive oil in a large heavy saucepan over low heat. Add garlic, onion and ginger; sauté until soft and golden, about 10 minutes, stirring frequently. Add carrots and parsnips; cook, covered, until vegetables are tender, about 10 minutes.

2. Add broth, salt and pepper. Bring to a boil over high heat; reduce heat and simmer 20 minutes.

3. Add shredded chicken and noodles; simmer until thoroughly heated.

PER SERVING: Calories 240; fat 8g; chol. 75mg; prot. 21g; carbs. 21g; fiber 3g; sodium 1150mg

oyster stew

This is the classic New England stew—it contains no thickening. Do not boil half-and-half as it will curdle. SERVES 6

3 tablespoons butter

1 cup finely chopped celery (about 4 stalks)

3 tablespoons finely chopped shallots

2 cups whole milk

2 cups half-and-half

2 (8-ounce) containers freshly shucked oysters, undrained

1 teaspoon Worcestershire sauce

½ teaspoon salt

½ teaspoon coarsely ground black pepper

⅛ teaspoon ground red pepper

Oyster crackers

Melt butter in a Dutch oven over medium heat. Add celery and shallots; cook until shallots are tender. Add milk and half-and-half; stir well. Heat until mixture is almost boiling. Add remaining ingredients; cook, stirring constantly, until edges of oysters curl. Remove from heat. Serve with oyster crackers.

PER SERVING: Calories 250; fat 19g; chol. 70mg; prot. 9g; carbs. 13g; fiber 0g; sodium 420mg

vegetable pork bowl

There's nothing quite as comforting or tasty as slurping a big bowl of Vietnamese pho on a cold day—unless it's this version studded with American flavors. Instead of beef and Asian noodles, we used a premarinated pork tenderloin, country ham, sweet potatoes and spinach for a decidedly New England taste. We added edamame (fresh soybeans) for a nutritious nod to our Asian neighbors. SERVES 6

4 ounces country ham (or bacon)

1 (1½-pound) hickory-smoked or honey-mustard-marinated pork tenderloin

2 onions, slivered

1 cup shelled edamame

2 small sweet potatoes, peeled and cubed

4 cups low-sodium chicken broth

3 cups spinach

1 pound whole-wheat spaghetti, cooked

¾ cup finely shredded Cheddar cheese

6 tablespoons chopped green onions

1.   Cook ham in a Dutch oven over medium-high heat 5 minutes; remove from pan. Add pork (with marinade) to pan; cook 20 minutes. Remove pork from pan; shred or chop into bite-sized pieces.

2.   Place onion in pan; sauté 5 minutes. Add pork, edamame, sweet potatoes and broth; bring to a boil, reduce heat and simmer 15 minutes. Stir in ham and spinach; cook 1 minute. Place pasta into 6 large bowls. Top with pork mixture, cheese and green onions.

PER SERVING: Calories 410; fat 9g; chol. 55mg; prot. 30g; carbs. 56g; fiber 10g; sodium 1110mg

saimin

You can prep the first three steps of this traditional Hawaiian noodle soup hours ahead. The final cooking will only take a couple of minutes. SERVES 4

8 ounces dried Chinese-style egg noodles

1 tablespoon dark sesame oil, plus more for drizzling

1 to 2 cups broccoli florets

4 cups low-sodium chicken broth

3 slices peeled fresh ginger

8 ounces extra-firm tofu, drained

2 tablespoons vegetable oil, divided

2 eggs, lightly beaten and seasoned with salt and pepper

1 teaspoon soy sauce

¼ teaspoon salt

Coarsely ground black pepper

¼ pound fresh snow peas, trimmed

1½ cups sliced bok choy or Napa cabbage

6 ounces cooked chicken or pork, chopped or shredded

1 cup fresh bean sprouts

2 green onions, thinly sliced on the bias

1. Cook noodles according to package directions. Drain well, rinse in cold water, and combine with 1 tablespoon sesame oil in a large bowl.

2. Cook broccoli in 3 cups of boiling water until crisp-tender, 2 to 3 minutes; drain. Rinse in cold water; drain.

3. Heat broth and ginger in a large saucepan over low heat about 30 minutes. Do not allow to boil; remove ginger.

4. Place tofu between paper towels until barely moist; cut into ½-inch-thick cubes. Heat 1 tablespoon vegetable oil in a large skillet over medium-high heat. Add tofu and cook on all sides until golden brown, 5 to 6 minutes. Remove tofu from pan; set aside on paper towels to drain.

5. Heat 1 tablespoon vegetable oil in pan. Add eggs and tilt pan to cover the bottom with a thin layer of egg. When egg has set, carefully turn it over. Slide egg crepe onto a plate; cool. Roll up crepe to form a tight cylinder and cut crosswise into thin strips.

6. Bring broth to a boil over medium-high heat. Add soy sauce, salt, pepper, snow peas and cabbage; cook 1 minute. Add noodles, broccoli, chicken, tofu, egg and sprouts; cook 30 seconds. Ladle into bowls; sprinkle with onions, drizzle with sesame oil and serve immediately.

PER SERVING: Calories 480; fat 17g; chol. 205mg; prot. 32g; carbs. 50g; fiber 5g; sodium 1050mg

to keep ginger fresh indefinitely, *peel it, chop it, and place it in a jar with some sherry. You'll have ginger whenever you need it—and some flavorful sherry as well.*

green bean salad with prosciutto di parma

arugula salad with strawberries and feta

cobb-style salad

green bean salad with prosciutto di parma

three bean salad with tomatoes and green onions

corn and tomato salad with lemon dressing

walnut beet salad

thai-style peanut cabbage salad

summer salad with okra

roasted chicken salad with basil

tabbouleh with chicken and corn

shrimp and fresh herb salad

thai beef salad

green goddess dressing

orange cumin vinaigrette

herb-infused olive oil

salads

arugula salad with strawberries and feta

Peppery arugula is a great contrast with sweet, ripe strawberries, especially when it's berry season. **SERVES 4**

VINAIGRETTE:

¼ cup lime juice

1 teaspoon honey

½ teaspoon kosher salt

¼ cup extra-virgin olive oil

Coarsely ground black pepper

SALAD:

6 cups arugula

2 cups halved strawberries

½ cup (2 ounces) crumbled feta cheese

1. To prepare vinaigrette, combine all ingredients in a jar; cover tightly and shake vigorously.

2. Divide arugula evenly among 4 salad plates; drizzle with vinaigrette. Arrange strawberries and feta over salad.

PER SERVING: Calories 220; fat 18g; chol. 15mg; prot. 4g; carbs. 10g; fiber 2g; sodium 460mg

cobb-style salad

Hollywood's Brown Derby Restaurant made this salad famous. The original consisted of chopped chicken, bacon, eggs, tomatoes, avocado, green onions, watercress, Cheddar and lettuce, tossed with a vinaigrette, and topped with a generous amount of Roquefort. **SERVES 6**

DRESSING:

⅓ cup extra-virgin olive oil

2 tablespoons red wine vinegar

2 teaspoons lemon juice

1 teaspoon Dijon mustard

½ teaspoon Worcestershire sauce

¼ teaspoon sugar

1 small garlic clove, crushed

½ teaspoon kosher salt

Coarsely ground black pepper

SALAD:

10 cups coarsely chopped lettuce (such as romaine and Boston)

2 medium tomatoes, chopped (abut 8 ounces)

1½ cups chopped, cooked chicken breast

6 bacon slices, cooked and crumbled

3 hard-cooked eggs, chopped

½ cup (2 ounces) crumbled Roquefort or blue cheese

1 diced peeled ripe avocado

1. To prepare dressing, combine all ingredients in a jar, cover tightly and shake vigorously.

2. To prepare salad, arrange lettuce on a large serving platter. Arrange tomatoes in a strip down the center of the platter; place chicken, bacon, eggs and cheese in strips on either side of tomatoes. Scatter avocado around edge of platter.

3. Before serving, slide the salad into a large bowl. Drizzle dressing over salad; toss gently to coat.

PER SERVING: Calories 330; fat 25g; chol. 150mg; prot. 21g; carbs. 8g; fiber 4g; sodium 420mg

green bean salad with prosciutto di parma

The rich flavor and silky texture of prosciutto di Parma, the most famous of the Italian hams, make a delicious addition to this summery salad. SERVES 4

1 pound green beans, trimmed and cut diagonally in half

1 medium yellow or zucchini squash, cut into thin strips

6 radishes, thinly sliced

2 ounces prosciutto di Parma, thinly sliced and cut into thin strips

2 tablespoons finely chopped fresh flat-leaf parsley

2 tablespoons extra-virgin olive oil

2 tablespoons red wine vinegar

½ teaspoon salt

Coarsely ground black pepper

Steam green beans until crisp-tender, 6 to 8 minutes. Pour into a colander and rinse with cold running water. Drain well, pat dry with paper towels and transfer to a large bowl. Add remaining ingredients and toss to combine.

PER SERVING: Calories 150; fat 9g; chol. 10mg; prot. 7g; carbs. 12g; fiber 5g; sodium 690mg

to keep cooked vegetables crisp *and bright for salads, plunge them in ice water after cooking.*

three bean salad with tomatoes and green onions

Fresh al dente green beans and cilantro update this bean salad favorite. SERVES 6

½ pound (1½ cups) green beans, trimmed and cut diagonally in thirds

1 (15½-ounce) can cannellini beans, rinsed and drained

1 (15½-ounce) can pinto beans, rinsed and drained

2 large plum tomatoes, diced (about 1½ cups)

5 green onions, thinly sliced

¼ cup finely chopped fresh cilantro

3 tablespoons extra-virgin olive oil

3 tablespoons red wine vinegar

½ teaspoon sugar

1 garlic clove, crushed

½ teaspoon salt

Coarsely ground black pepper

1. Steam green beans, covered, until crisp-tender, 5 to 7 minutes. Rinse under cold water; drain well.

2. Combine green beans, cannellini and pinto beans, tomatoes, green onions and cilantro in a large bowl.

3. Place remaining ingredients in a small bowl; stir with a whisk. Drizzle oil mixture over salad; stir gently.

PER SERVING: Calories 200; fat 8g; chol. 0mg; prot. 8g; carbs. 25g; fiber 8g; sodium 490mg

corn and tomato salad with lemon dressing

Toss this fresh salad together up to a day ahead. Serve on a bed of arugula or lettuce. **SERVES 6**

2 cups cooked fresh or frozen corn

**1 medium zucchini,
diced (about 1 cup)**

2 cups coarsely chopped tomato

2 tablespoons chopped fresh mint

2 tablespoons extra-virgin olive oil

2 tablespoons lemon juice

1 teaspoon honey

½ teaspoon salt

Coarsely ground black pepper

Combine corn, zucchini, tomato and mint in a large bowl. Place remaining ingredients in a medium a bowl; stir well with a whisk. Pour dressing over salad; mix gently.

PER SERVING: Calories 120; fat 5g; chol. 0mg; prot. 3g; carbs. 17g; fiber 3g; sodium 360mg

walnut beet salad

Roast and dice the beets and make the vinaigrette up to three days in advance. SERVES 8

2 to 3 medium to large beets, scrubbed and trimmed

VINAIGRETTE:

2 tablespoons raisins

¼ cup cider vinegar

1½ teaspoons honey

½ teaspoon Dijon mustard

¼ teaspoon salt

½ cup walnut or vegetable oil

SALAD:

1 pound spring greens

1 head romaine, separated into leaves, and sliced into 1½ inch wide strips

3 green onions, chopped

¾ cup (3 ounces) walnut pieces, toasted

1 cup (4 ounces) crumbled blue cheese

1 crisp tart apple (such as Granny Smith), diced

1. Preheat oven to 400F.

2. Wrap beets in foil. Place on a baking sheet; bake 30 to 45 minutes or until tender. Cool slightly. Rinse with cold water; rub off skins. Dice beets; set aside 2 tablespoons diced beets for vinaigrette. Set aside remaining beets for salad.

3. To prepare vinaigrette, place raisins in a heatproof bowl. Bring vinegar to a boil in a small saucepan; pour over raisins. Let stand 30 minutes or until raisins are plump and liquid is cool. Transfer to a food processor; process until raisins form a dark paste. Add 2 tablespoons diced beets, honey, mustard and salt. With processor on, slowly add oil through food chute; process until well blended. Transfer vinaigrette to a small bowl; refrigerate until ready to use. Return to room temperature and stir well before using.

4. To prepare salad, combine greens, romaine and onions in a large salad bowl; toss well. Add walnuts, beets, blue cheese and apple. Drizzle vinaigrette over salad; toss well.

PER SERVING: Calories 290; fat 25g; chol. 10mg; prot. 6g; carbs. 13g; fiber 4g; sodium 360mg

thai-style peanut cabbage salad

Most cultures love peanuts. In fact, they play an integral role in Thai dishes, such as this crunchy, spunky salad. **SERVES 6**

DRESSING:

⅓ cup packed brown sugar

2 tablespoons peanut oil

4 garlic cloves, peeled and chopped

½ teaspoon crushed red pepper

2 tablespoons low-sodium soy sauce

¼ cup lime juice

2 tablespoons water

1 teaspoon finely grated peeled fresh ginger

¼ teaspoon salt

SALAD:

¼ pound blanched green beans

4 cups baby spinach (about 4 ounces)

2 cups very thinly sliced green cabbage

3 green onions, sliced

½ red pepper, thinly sliced

⅔ cup chopped dry-roasted peanuts, toasted if desired

¼ cup chopped fresh basil or mint

1 (1-ounce) package roasted vegetable chips or sweet potato chips (such as Terra), lightly crushed

1. To prepare dressing, combine all ingredients in a jar. Cover tightly; shake vigorously.

2. To prepare salad, place beans and next 4 ingredients (beans through pepper) in a large bowl. Just before serving, drizzle about two-thirds of dressing over salad; toss to coat well. Sprinkle with peanuts, herbs and vegetable chips. Serve with remaining dressing.

PER SERVING: Calories 240; fat 15g; chol. 0mg; prot. 7g; carbs. 22g; fiber 7g; sodium 620mg

toasting nuts increases their flavor exponentially.
To toast, place nuts on a baking sheet and bake at 375F for 10 minutes or until browned.

summer salad with okra

Crunchy raw okra is a welcome addition to this summer salad.   SERVES 4

**1 cup small okra pods,
cut in half vertically**

**1 (5-ounce) package
mixed salad greens**

1 small red bell pepper, thinly sliced

**½ peeled jicama, thinly
sliced and cut into strips**

¼ teaspoon kosher salt

Coarsely ground black pepper

**¼ cup poppy seed dressing
(or other sweet dressing)**

Place all ingredients except dressing into a medium bowl; toss. Serve immediately with your choice of dressing.

PER SERVING: Calories 130; fat 6g; chol. 5mg; prot. 3g; carbs. 15g; fiber 6g; sodium 300mg

roasted chicken salad with basil

A purchased rotisserie chicken makes this salad a snap. Cook the corn and beans until just crisp-tender. **SERVES 8**

1 (2½ to 3-pound) rotisserie chicken

1¾ cups cooked green beans, cut into 1-inch pieces

1¾ cups cooked corn kernels (about 3 ears)

1 red bell pepper, chopped (about 5 ounces)

½ cup chopped fresh basil

¼ cup (1 ounce) pine nuts, toasted

2 garlic cloves, crushed

⅓ cup extra-virgin olive oil

¼ cup red or white wine vinegar

1 teaspoon salt

½ teaspoon coarsely ground black pepper

1. Remove and discard skin from chicken. Remove chicken from bones; shred meat into bite-sized pieces.

2. Place chicken and next 5 ingredients (chicken through pine nuts) in a large bowl; stir gently to combine.

3. Place remaining ingredients in a medium bowl; stir well with a whisk. Immediately pour over salad; toss gently to coat.

PER SERVING: Calories 320; fat 19g; chol. 75mg; prot. 27g; carbs. 10g; fiber 2g; sodium 370mg

tabbouleh with chicken and corn

Tabbouleh, the lemony Middle Eastern bulgur salad with fresh mint and lots of chopped parsley, is transformed into a main dish with chicken and corn. Store-bought or leftover cooked chicken works fine. SERVES 4

¾ cup uncooked bulgur

Boiling water

1½ cups chopped, cooked chicken breast

1 cup cooked corn kernels

1 cup finely chopped fresh flat-leaf parsley

2 tablespoons finely chopped fresh mint

3 tablespoons lemon juice

3 tablespoons extra-virgin olive oil

2 tablespoons orange juice

¾ teaspoon salt

Coarsely ground black pepper

1.   Place bulgur in a large bowl; cover with boiling water to 1 inch above bulgur. Let stand, covered, 30 minutes or until bulgur is softened. Transfer to a strainer and press down with a spoon to remove water.

2.   Return bulgur to bowl; add chicken, corn, parsley and mint.

3.   Combine remaining ingredients in a small bowl; stir with a whisk. Drizzle over salad; mix gently.

PER SERVING: Calories 280; fat 10g; chol. 45mg; prot. 21g; carbs. 29g; fiber 7g; sodium 505mg

shrimp and fresh herb salad

Use any combination of fresh herbs you like. Shrimp is delicious with almost any fresh herb.

SERVES 6

2 pounds cooked shrimp, peeled and chopped

1 cup grape tomato halves

¾ cup light mayonnaise

1 tablespoon Dijon mustard

1 teaspoon lemon juice

2 tablespoons chopped fresh parsley

2 tablespoons chopped fresh dill, chives or tarragon

Combine all ingredients in a medium bowl; stir gently.

PER SERVING: Calories 290; fat 13g; chol. 315mg; prot. 38g; carbs. 4g; fiber 0g; sodium 720mg

in place of flowers,
cut fresh herbs and place in a jar of water for a pretty table decoration. Then chop and toss them into your favorite dish.

thai beef salad

This main course salad captures the essence of Thai cuisine. Full of contrasting textures (crisp greens, tender beef, crunchy peanuts) and tossed with a vibrant dressing, it's a bright, healthful dish that's alive with flavor. SERVES 4

¼ cup lime juice

3 tablespoons fish sauce

1 tablespoon, plus 1 teaspoon, dark brown sugar

1 serrano or jalapeño, seeded and finely chopped

1¼ pounds flank steak

2 teaspoons peanut oil

Coarsely ground black pepper

6 cups torn romaine lettuce

1 small red onion, halved and thinly sliced

½ English cucumber, halved lengthwise and sliced

¼ cup roughly chopped fresh mint, divided

3 tablespoons roughly chopped fresh cilantro, divided

⅓ cup coarsely chopped unsalted peanuts

1. Combine first four ingredients in a small bowl; whisk.

2. Prepare grill or preheat broiler. Brush steak with peanut oil; season with pepper. Grill or broil, turning once, until medium rare, about 5 minutes per side. Remove from heat and let stand 10 minutes.

3. Combine romaine, red onion, cucumber, and half the mint and cilantro in a large bowl. Add all but 2 tablespoons of lime juice mixture. Toss well and mound on a large serving platter.

4. Thinly slice steak across the grain, and toss with remaining lime juice mixture. Arrange steak on top of salad. Sprinkle with remaining mint and cilantro and chopped peanuts.

PER SERVING: Calories 370; fat 18g; chol. 60mg; prot. 37g; carbs. 15g; fiber 4g; sodium 1120mg

green goddess dressing

Use the dressing as a sauce for fish and shellfish for a refreshing addition to simple fare.

SERVES 16

1 cup mayonnaise

2 green onions, finely chopped

2 tablespoons finely chopped fresh parsley

2 teaspoons anchovy paste

1 teaspoon white wine vinegar

¾ teaspoon finely chopped fresh or ¼ teaspoon dried tarragon

¼ teaspoon coarsely ground black pepper

Stir all ingredients together in a medium bowl until evenly blended.

PER (1-TABLESPOON) SERVING: Calories 100; fat 11g; chol. 5mg; prot. 0g; carbs. 0g; fiber 0g; sodium 230mg

for more interesting salads, *try some of the new greens available—arugula, endive, frissée, radicchio.*

orange cumin vinaigrette

This sweet-tart dressing is great over bitter greens. **SERVES 12**

1 tablespoon chopped fresh cilantro

1 garlic clove, minced

¼ teaspoon ground cumin

¼ teaspoon crushed red pepper

¼ cup extra-virgin olive oil

2 tablespoons honey

3 tablespoons lime juice

¼ cup fresh orange juice

Combine all ingredients in a jar. Cover tightly; shake vigorously. Serve over mixed greens.

PER (1-TABLESPOON) SERVING: Calories 55; fat 5g; chol. 0mg; prot. 0g; carbs. 4g; fiber 0g; sodium 5mg

herb-infused olive oil

Here's a flavorful oil that'll make your salads pop all summer. Or use it as a finishing oil, drizzled lightly over sautéed pork cutlets, grilled vegetables, or salted, sliced tomatoes.
SERVES 16.

1 cup extra-virgin olive oil

1 large rosemary sprig, cut into 2-inch pieces

2 oregano sprigs

2 thyme sprigs

2 dried hot red chiles

1 garlic clove, peeled and quartered

1. Place ingredients in a large jar; cover tightly. Let stand at room temperature at least 2 days before serving, or keep in refrigerator up to 2 weeks.

2. Bring oil to room temperature and strain before serving; discard solids.

PER (1-TABLESPOON) SERVING: Calories 130; fat 14g; chol. 0mg; prot. 0g; carbs. 0g; fiber 0g; sodium 10mg

maple-glazed brussels sprouts

prosciutto-wrapped asparagus bundles

green bean and tomato sauté

garlic-braised broccoli rabe

maple-glazed brussels sprouts

stir-fried chard with asian seasonings

chard with lemon and feta

quick okra sauté

bacon mashed potatoes

gratin of sweet potatoes and swiss chard

chipotle cheese grits

cilantro lime rice

spanish rice

quinoa, spinach and walnut stir-fry

cilantro chimichurri

cucumber mango relish

roasted red pepper pesto

all-purpose asian marinade

dry rubs for fish

rosemary biscuits

rosy swirl cranberry bread

onion focaccia

sides

prosciutto-wrapped asparagus bundles

Wrapped tightly around bundles of asparagus spears, the salty prosciutto crisps on the grill.

SERVES 8

1 pound asparagus, trimmed

1 tablespoon extra-virgin olive oil

¼ teaspoon salt

Coarsely ground black pepper

1 (3-ounce) package thinly sliced prosciutto di Parma or country ham

Cooking spray

1. Prepare grill.

2. Toss asparagus with oil, salt and pepper. Wrap 2 or 3 asparagus spears with a slice of prosciutto to form a bundle. Repeat with remaining asparagus and prosciutto. Place on grill rack coated with cooking spray. Grill 5 to 10 minutes, turning once.

PER SERVING: Calories 50; fat 3g; chol. 10mg; prot. 4g; carbs. 2g; fiber 1g; sodium 360mg

green bean and tomato sauté

Herbs and tomatoes dress up a classic green bean side. **SERVES 6**

1½ pounds green beans, trimmed and halved crosswise

1¼ teaspoons salt

2 tablespoons extra-virgin olive oil, divided

3 garlic cloves, minced and divided

1 large shallot, finely chopped

1 cup grape tomatoes, halved

1 tablespoon sugar

1 tablespoon balsamic vinegar

½ teaspoon dried marjoram

½ teaspoon dried basil

¼ teaspoon coarsely ground black pepper

1. Place green beans in a large saucepan. Cover with water. Add ½ teaspoon salt. Bring to a boil and cook 3 minutes; drain.

2. Heat oil in a large nonstick skillet over medium-high heat. Add garlic and shallot; cook 2 minutes. Add tomatoes and sugar; cook until just beginning to wilt, about 2 minutes. Stir in green beans, vinegar, marjoram and basil; cook until thoroughly heated, about 2 minutes. Transfer to a bowl and keep warm. Sprinkle with remaining salt and pepper.

PER SERVING: Calories 90; fat 5g; chol. 0mg; prot. 2g; carbs. 12g; fiber 4g; sodium 300mg

garlic-braised broccoli rabe

Broccoli rabe is related to both the cabbage and turnip families. The leaves have a pungent, slightly bitter flavor. Cook broccoli rabe much the same way as you cook broccoli. **SERVES 8**

2 medium bunches broccoli rabe (rapini), about 1 pound, trimmed and coarsely chopped

2 tablespoons olive oil

2 garlic cloves, sliced

½ teaspoon salt

Coarsely ground black pepper

1. Place broccoli rabe in a large saucepan; cover with water. Bring to a boil and cook 2 minutes; drain well.

2. Heat oil in a large skillet over medium heat. Add garlic; sauté 3 minutes. Add broccoli rabe, salt and pepper; sauté 2 minutes.

PER SERVING: Calories 70; fat 5g; chol. 0mg; prot. 2g; carbs. 3g; fiber 0g; sodium 160 mg

maple-glazed brussels sprouts

Brussels sprouts are quickly steamed, then quickly stir-fried with an Asian-inspired maple glaze. **SERVES 6**

1½ pounds Brussels sprouts, trimmed and halved

1 tablespoon soy sauce

1 tablespoon Dijon mustard

¼ cup maple syrup

¼ teaspoon salt

⅛ teaspoon coarsely ground black pepper

1 tablespoon vegetable oil

1 small onion, thinly sliced

1 red bell pepper, thinly sliced

1. Steam Brussels sprouts, covered, until crisp-tender, about 3 minutes. Drain and rinse with cold water; drain.

2. Place soy sauce and next 4 ingredients (soy sauce through black pepper) in a medium bowl; whisk to combine.

3. Heat oil in a heavy nonstick skillet over medium-high heat. Sauté onion and bell pepper 5 minutes; add Brussels sprouts and continue to cook 4 minutes.

4. Add soy sauce mixture to pan. Cook until vegetables are coated and glaze thickens, about 2 minutes. Serve immediately.

PER SERVING: Calories 120; fat 3g; chol. 0mg; prot. 5g; carbs. 23g; fiber 5g; sodium 379mg

> if you love cooking with maple syrup, *molasses or honey, give sorghum a try. It's super high in antioxidants and adds a great caramel taste to any recipe calling for honey.*

stir-fried chard with asian seasonings

Here's an easy way to add flavor to these hearty, oh-so-good-for-you greens—delicious with roast chicken, pork or beef. **SERVES 4**

1 tablespoon vegetable oil

2 garlic cloves, minced

1½ pounds Swiss chard, trimmed and coarsely chopped

2 teaspoons soy sauce

½ teaspoon sesame oil

3 drops hot pepper sauce (such as Tabasco)

1.   Heat oil in a large nonstick skillet over medium-high heat. Add garlic and cook 1 minute.

2.   Gradually add chard; as one batch wilts, add another. Cook over medium heat, stirring frequently, until tender and most of the liquid evaporates, about 10 minutes. Add remaining ingredients and stir to combine.

PER SERVING: Calories 70; fat 5g; chol. 0mg; prot. 3g; carbs. 7g; fiber 3g; sodium 580mg

chard with lemon and feta

The bright flavors of lemon and feta are perfect complements to earthy chard. This is especially nice served with grilled entrées. **SERVES 4**

1½ pounds Swiss chard, trimmed and coarsely chopped

1 tablespoon butter

2 teaspoons lemon juice

½ cup (2 ounces) crumbled feta cheese

¼ teaspoon salt

Coarsely ground black pepper

1. Rinse chard and place in a large stockpot with water still clinging to leaves.

2. Cover and cook over medium heat until tender, about 10 minutes.

3. Drain well and return to pan. Reduce heat to low. Add remaining ingredients; toss to combine.

PER SERVING: Calories 110; fat 7g; chol. 25mg; prot. 6g; carbs. 7g; fiber 3g; sodium 740mg

quick okra sauté

To those familiar only with fried okra, this will be an okra epiphany. With its crisp, green, fresh taste, you'll swear you're eating a different vegetable. Sauté only until al dente. Small, tender pods are best in this simple sauté. **SERVES 2**

2 teaspoons olive oil

1 teaspoon butter

½ pound small okra pods

¼ teaspoon kosher salt

Coarsely ground black pepper

Heat oil and butter in a large skillet over high heat. Add okra; sauté until pods are bright green with some light browning, 5 to 6 minutes. Sprinkle with salt and pepper; serve hot.

PER SERVING: Calories 90; fat 7g; chol. 5mg; prot. 2g; carbs. 8g; fiber 4g; sodium 310mg

bacon mashed potatoes

Perfect for special occasions, these rich potatoes contain creamy Neufchatel cheese, butter and bacon. **SERVES 8**

3 pounds Yukon Gold potatoes, peeled and chopped

1 (8-ounce) block Neufchatel cheese, softened

¼ cup butter, softened

1 teaspoon salt

Coarsely ground black pepper

½ cup 2% reduced-fat milk, if needed

6 thick-cut bacon slices, cooked and crumbled

6 green onions, chopped

1. Place potatoes in a large saucepan; cover with cold water. Bring to a boil. Reduce heat and simmer until tender, about 15 minutes; drain.

2. Return potatoes to pan; add cheese, butter, salt and pepper. Beat with a mixer at medium speed, or mash with a potato masher until smooth. For a thinner consistency, add milk. Top potatoes with bacon and green onion before serving.

PER SERVING: Calories 320; fat 16g; chol. 45mg; prot. 11g; carbs. 33g; fiber 2g; sodium 660mg

gratin of sweet potatoes and swiss chard

For cooks in a hurry, 2 (10-ounce) packages of frozen chopped spinach, thawed and with the water squeezed out, can be substituted for the chard. Parboiling the potatoes ensures they'll be done quickly. **SERVES 6**

2 pounds peeled sweet potatoes, cut into ¼-inch-thick slices

1 pound Swiss chard, trimmed and coarsely chopped

3 tablespoons butter

3 tablespoons all-purpose flour

1½ cups 2% reduced-fat milk

1½ cups low-sodium chicken broth

1 teaspoon kosher salt

¼ teaspoon ground nutmeg

⅛ teaspoon coarsely ground black pepper

3 tablespoons grated Parmigiano-Reggiano cheese

⅔ cup fresh breadcrumbs

1. Preheat oven to 400F. Butter an 11 x 7-inch baking dish or a 2½-quart gratin dish.

2. Place potatoes in a large saucepan; cover with water. Bring to a boil, cover, reduce heat, and simmer until tender, about 5 minutes; drain.

3. Rinse chard and place in the same saucepan with water clinging to leaves; cover and cook over medium heat until tender, about 5 minutes. Drain thoroughly.

4. Melt butter in the same saucepan; add flour and whisk to combine. Gradually add milk and broth, stirring with a whisk until blended. Cook over medium heat, stirring occasionally, until mixture comes to a boil. Reduce heat; simmer 2 minutes, stirring constantly. Stir in salt, nutmeg and pepper.

5. Arrange half the potatoes in prepared baking dish. Top with chard and half the sauce. Cover with remaining potatoes and sauce. Sprinkle with cheese and breadcrumbs. Bake 25 minutes or until golden brown and bubbling.

PER SERVING: Calories 300; fat 9g; chol. 25mg; prot. 9g; carbs. 48g; fiber 6g; sodium 920mg

chipotle cheese grits

Chipotle peppers are smoked jalapeños that are often sold packed in adobo sauce, a thick purée of tomatoes, onions, garlic and vinegar. **SERVES 4**

3 cups water

¾ cup quick-cooking grits

¼ teaspoon salt

1 cup (4 ounces) shredded extra-sharp white Cheddar cheese

1 chipotle chile in adobo sauce, mashed

Bring water to a boil in a medium saucepan; stir in grits and salt. Cover, reduce heat and simmer until thickened, about 5 minutes, stirring twice. Remove from heat; stir in cheese and chile.

PER SERVING: Calories 220; fat 10g; chol. 30mg; prot. 9g; carbs. 25g; fiber 1g; sodium 610mg

cilantro lime rice

The simple addition of lime and cilantro is all that it takes to make this rice become your new standard. **SERVES 4**

1½ tablespoons olive oil

1 cup dry long-grain rice

2 cups low-sodium chicken broth

¼ teaspoon salt

½ cup chopped fresh cilantro

Grated rind of 1 medium lime

Juice of 1 medium lime

Heat oil in a medium saucepan over medium heat; add rice and stir to coat. Add broth and salt. Bring to a boil over high heat; stir. Cover, reduce heat and simmer over medium-low heat 20 minutes. Remove from heat; let stand 10 minutes. Fluff rice with a fork and stir in lime rind, juice and cilantro.

PER SERVING: Calories 210; fat 5g; chol. 0mg; prot. 4g; carbs. 36g; fiber 0g; sodium 300mg

spanish rice

Spanish rice is prepared by browning rice with onions and garlic before cooking it in chicken broth. The green beans may be doubled, if desired. **SERVES 4**

2 tablespoons olive oil

½ onion, finely chopped (about ½ cup)

1 garlic clove, minced

1 small tomato, finely chopped

¼ cup diced green beans

1 cup uncooked long-grain rice

½ teaspoon salt

½ teaspoon dried oregano

2 cups low-sodium chicken broth

1. Heat olive oil in a large skillet over medium heat. Add onion and garlic; cook 3 minutes, stirring occasionally. Add tomato and beans; cook 3 minutes. Add rice, salt and oregano and continue cooking and stirring until rice is lightly browned, about 1 minute. Add broth; bring to a boil over medium-high heat. Cover, reduce heat, and simmer until liquid is absorbed, 15 to 20 minutes.

2. Remove from heat; let stand 5 minutes. Fluff with a fork before serving.

PER SERVING: Calories 240; fat 7g; chol. 5mg; prot. 5g; carbs. 40g; fiber 1g; sodium 590mg

the best of relish cookbook

quinoa, spinach and walnut stir-fry

This recipe stars quinoa (keen-wa), a whole grain that's a complete protein, fiber-rich and chock-full of vitamins and minerals. Substitute couscous if you can't find quinoa. Toast the walnuts in the oven for 5 minutes and they'll impart a lot of flavor to this dish. **SERVES 4**

1 cup quinoa

1 tablespoon olive oil

1 teaspoon minced garlic

½ teaspoon salt

2 cups water

5 ounces fresh baby spinach

1 cup grape or cherry tomatoes, halved

½ cup walnut pieces, toasted

½ cup freshly grated Parmigiano-Reggiano cheese

Basil leaves

1.   Place quinoa in small bowl, add water to cover, and swish to rinse. Pour into fine mesh strainer and drain well.

2.   Heat oil in large skillet. Add quinoa. Cook, stirring, over medium heat until golden, about 10 minutes. Add garlic and cook, stirring, 1 minute. Add salt and 2 cups of water. Bring to a boil. Reduce heat; cover and cook over medium-low until water is absorbed, about 15 minutes.

3.   Add spinach and tomatoes. Cook over medium heat until spinach is almost wilted and tomatoes are warmed, about 1 minute. Stir in walnuts and cheese. Garnish with basil leaves.

PER SERVING: Calories 36; fat 19g; chol. 37mg; prot. 13g; carbs. 37g; fiber 6g; sodium 510mg

cilantro chimichurri

The Latin pesto known as chimichurri has as many renditions as there are cooks. This version incorporates cilantro and resembles the chimichurri most often found in Central America. Use it as a marinade and basting sauce as well as a condiment. **MAKES 1 CUP, ENOUGH FOR 6 STEAKS**

6 garlic cloves

1 cup fresh cilantro

1 cup flat-leaf parsley

½ cup chopped onion

2 tablespoons white wine vinegar

½ teaspoon dried oregano

½ teaspoon crushed red pepper

½ cup extra-virgin olive oil

½ teaspoon salt

Coarsely ground black pepper

Place garlic in food processor; process until finely chopped. Add cilantro and next 5 ingredients (cilantro through crushed red pepper). Add olive oil in a thin stream through food chute and process until smooth; add salt and pepper. Cover and refrigerate up to 1 week. Serve with grilled steak.

PER SERVING: Calories 180; fat 19g; chol. 0mg; prot. 1g; carbs. 3g; fiber 1g; sodium 200mg

cucumber mango relish

Seasoned rice vinegar is rice vinegar with sugar and salt added. For peak flavors and texture, serve this relish the same day it is assembled. **SERVES 4**

1 cup diced peeled English cucumber

1 cup diced mango

2 tablespoons chopped fresh cilantro

1 tablespoon finely chopped red onion

3 tablespoons seasoned rice vinegar

Combine all ingredients in a medium bowl; mix well. Chill.

PER SERVING: Calories 10; fat 0g; chol. 0mg; prot. 1g; carbs. 2g; fiber 1g; sodium 2mg

roasted red pepper pesto

Try basting with this sauce as well as serving it alongside grilled meats, seafood and veggies. Or spread it on grilled bread. It can be made and refrigerated up to 3 weeks in advance. **SERVES 8**

2 large red bell peppers (about 12 ounces)

⅓ cup chopped walnuts (about 1½ ounces)

2 garlic cloves, minced

3 tablespoons extra-virgin olive oil

½ teaspoon salt

1. Preheat broiler.

2. Cut peppers in half lengthwise; discard seeds and membranes. Place pepper halves, skin side up, on a foil-lined baking sheet; flatten with hand. Broil 20 minutes or until blackened. Place peppers in a zip-top plastic bag; seal. Let stand 20 minutes or until slightly cool.

3. Peel peppers. Place peppers and remaining ingredients in a blender or food processor; process until smooth.

PER SERVING: Calories 90; fat 9g; chol. 0mg; prot. 1g; carbs. 3g; fiber 1g; sodium 150mg

all-purpose asian marinade

For added kick, add the jalapeno seeds. This makes enough marinade for 2 pounds of chicken, fish, beef or pork. **MAKES ABOUT 1 CUP**

⅓ cup lime juice

3 tablespoons fish sauce

¼ cup low-sodium soy sauce

2 tablespoons vegetable oil

2 tablespoons honey

3 garlic cloves, minced

1 jalapeño, seeded and chopped

Chopped fresh cilantro or basil

Combine all ingredients in a jar; shake well. Cover and chill up to 2 weeks.

PER SERVING: Calories 60; fat 3.5g; chol. 0mg; prot. 1g; carbs. 6g; fiber 0g; sodium 820mg

dry rubs for fish

Each of these rubs is enough for 2 pounds of fish, but you can double or triple the recipe and save the rest for the next time you grill. To use, lightly rub the fish with a little liquid (wine, broth, apple juice, lemon juice, soy sauce, etc.), then gently massage the rub onto the fish and let it stand at room temperature while the grill heats up.

CAJUN RUB

1½ teaspoons garlic powder

1½ teaspoons onion powder

1½ teaspoons dried thyme

1½ teaspoons dried oregano

1½ teaspoons paprika

1 teaspoon salt

¼ teaspoon celery seeds

¼ teaspoon ground red pepper

VIETNAMESE RUB

1 tablespoon light brown sugar

1 tablespoon black pepper

1 teaspoon salt

1 teaspoon ground ginger

½ teaspoon onion powder

¼ teaspoon garlic powder

MOROCCAN RUB

1 teaspoon salt

1 tablespoon ground ginger

1 teaspoon ground cumin

1 tablespoon ground coriander

1 teaspoon ground cinnamon

the best of relish cookbook

rosemary biscuits

This new take on a Southern quick bread is flavored with fresh rosemary. **MAKES 15 BISCUITS**

Cooking spray

2 cups all-purpose flour

4 teaspoons baking powder

¼ teaspoon baking soda

¾ teaspoon salt

1 tablespoon chopped
fresh rosemary

4 tablespoons butter or shortening

1 cup cold buttermilk

1. Preheat oven to 425F. Lightly coat a baking sheet with cooking spray.

2. Combine flour and next 4 ingredients (flour through rosemary) in a medium bowl.

3. Cut in butter with a pastry blender or 2 knives until mixture resembles coarse meal. Add buttermilk; stir just until moist. Turn dough out on floured surface and dust top of mixture with flour. Knead lightly 5 times. Roll into a 1-inch-thick round. Cut with 2-inch flour-dusted cutter. Place close together on baking sheet. Bake 15 minutes or until golden.

PER BISCUIT: Calories 90; fat 3.5g fat; chol .10mg; prot. 2g; carbs. 13g; fiber 0g; sodium 320mg

rosy swirl cranberry bread

This yeast-risen, homey-looking bread is grainy with a delectable jam-like swirl in the middle, featuring fresh cranberries. **MAKES 2 LOAVES (12 SLICES EACH)**

BREAD:

1 cup 2% reduced-fat milk

½ cup butter, divided

1 cup old-fashioned oats

2 (.25-ounce) packages dry yeast

1 cup warm water

2 eggs

2 teaspoons vanilla extract

3 tablespoons sugar

1 tablespoon salt

3 cups whole wheat flour

3 cups all-purpose flour, divided

Cooking spray

1 tablespoon cinnamon mixed with 3 tablespoons sugar

CRANBERRY FILLING:

1⅔ cups fresh cranberries

½ cup sugar

1. To prepare bread, combine milk and ¼ cup butter in a small saucepan; heat until butter melts. Pour into a large bowl and stir in oats. Let stand about 10 minutes.

2. Sprinkle yeast over warm water; let stand 10 minutes or until bubbly.

3. Add eggs, vanilla, sugar, salt and yeast mixture to oat mixture. Stir well.

4. Stir in whole wheat flour and 2 cups all-purpose flour, 1 cup at a time. Turn dough out onto a clean, floured surface; knead in remaining all-purpose flour, ¼-cup at a time, until smooth and pliable. Knead about 6 minutes. Coat a large bowl with cooking spray and place dough in it. Cover and let rise until doubled in bulk, 1 to 1½ hours.

5. To prepare filling, combine cranberries and sugar in a small saucepan. Cook, stirring constantly, until sugar melts and cranberries start to pop. Remove from heat and set aside.

6. Coat two 9 x 5-inch loaf pans with cooking spray. When dough has risen, punch it down; divide into two equal parts.

7. Melt ¼ cup butter. Roll out one portion of dough into a 12 x 16-inch rectangle on a floured surface. Brush with 2 tablespoons melted butter. Sprinkle on 2 tablespoons cinnamon-sugar, stopping ¾ inch from edges. Spread with half the cranberry filling, stopping ¾ inch from edges.

8. Roll dough up, starting on one of the short sides. Pinch seams together at both ends; tuck ends under slightly. Place loaf, seam side down, into prepared pan. Repeat for second loaf.

9. Cover loaves and let rise until doubled in bulk, 45 to 60 minutes.

10. Preheat oven to 375F. Bake 35 minutes or until bread is browned on bottom and sounds hollow when tapped. Remove from oven, let stand in pans 5 minutes, then remove from pans and cool on racks 30 minutes.

PER SLICE: Calories 180; fat 5g; chol. 30 mg; prot. 5g; carbs. 31g; fiber 3g; sodium 320mg

onion focaccia

Serve this with a big salad topped with chicken to make a complete meal. **SERVES 12**

4½ cups all-purpose flour, divided

**½ cup (2 ounces) grated
Parmigiano-Reggiano cheese**

1 teaspoon kosher salt

1 teaspoon dried rosemary, crushed

**1 (.25-ounce) package
quick-rise yeast**

1½ cups warm water (120F to 130F)

3 tablespoons olive oil, divided

Cooking spray

Cornmeal

3 leeks (about 1½ pounds)

8 green onions, trimmed

Coarsely ground sea salt

1. Combine 3½ cups flour and next 4 ingredients (flour through yeast) in a food processor; pulse 2 times or until blended. With processor on, slowly add water and 2 tablespoons oil through food chute; process until dough forms a ball.

2. Turn out onto a lightly floured surface; knead 5 minutes or until smooth and elastic, adding additional flour as necessary. Place dough in a large bowl coated with cooking spray. Turn dough to coat top; cover and let rise in a warm place, 1 hour.

3. Punch down dough; turn out onto a lightly floured surface. Divide into 2 pieces, shaping each into a 12-inch circle. Place on two large baking sheets coated with cooking spray and dusted with cornmeal. Cover and let rise until doubled in bulk, about 40 minutes.

4. Preheat oven to 450F.

5. Uncover dough. Gently brush 1 tablespoon olive oil over dough. Make indentations in top of dough using the handle of a wooden spoon or your fingertips.

6. Remove roots, outer leaves and tops from leeks. Rinse with cold water; cut into rounds. Arrange leek slices and green onions over top of dough. Sprinkle with sea salt

7. Bake 20 minutes or until golden; cool on wire racks. Remove focaccia to cutting board; cut in wedges.

PER SERVING: Calories 210; fat 4g; chol. 5mg; prot. 7g; carbs. 37g; fiber 2g; sodium 320mg

muffaletta

sandwiches

sliced egg and tomato sandwiches with dill mayonnaise

Sharp and distinctive arugula leaves add wonderful flavor to these simple summer sandwiches. SERVES 2

¼ cup light mayonnaise

1½ teaspoons chopped fresh dill

¼ teaspoon salt

Coarsely ground black pepper

4 slices whole-grain bread

2 hard-cooked eggs, thinly sliced

2 small tomatoes, thinly sliced

Arugula leaves

1.   Combine mayonnaise, dill, salt and pepper in a small bowl. Spread 2 tablespoons mayonnaise mixture over 2 bread slices. Layer each slice with half the egg slices, tomato slices and arugula.

2.   Spread 2 tablespoons mayonnaise mixture over remaining bread slices; place on top of sandwiches. Cut each sandwich in half diagonally.

PER SERVING: Calories 340; fat 17g; chol. 225mg; prot. 15g; carbs. 31g; fiber 5g; sodium 830mg

hot brown

This main dish sandwich, made famous at the Brown Hotel in Louisville, Kentucky, provides almost half of the calcium you need for the day. SERVES 2

2 tablespoons butter

2 tablespoons all-purpose flour

1½ cups 2% reduced-fat milk, heated

1 egg yolk

6 tablespoons (1½ ounces) grated Parmigiano-Reggiano cheese, divided

⅛ teaspoon kosher salt

Coarsely ground black pepper

4 slices white bread, toasted

8 ounces thinly sliced cooked turkey breast

Paprika

4 bacon slices, cooked

2 small tomatoes, cut into wedges

1. Melt butter in a medium saucepan over medium-low heat. Add flour; stir with a whisk to combine. Gradually add milk, stirring constantly with a whisk. Cook over medium heat until sauce thickens and comes to a boil; stirring constantly. Reduce heat to low, add egg yolk, ¼ cup Parmesan, salt and pepper. Cook and stir 2 minutes.

2. Preheat broiler.

3. Place one slice of toast on an ovenproof serving plate. Cut another slice of toast diagonally in half; arrange on either side of toast on plate. Place half the turkey on toast; pour half the sauce over sandwich. Sprinkle with paprika and 1 tablespoon cheese. Repeat with remaining sandwich ingredients on another ovenproof plate. Broil until lightly browned and bubbly. Place 2 slices of bacon on top of each sandwich; sprinkle with tomatoes.

PER SERVING: Calories 690; fat 31g; chol. 260mg; prot. 55g; carbs. 48g; fiber 3g; sodium 1900mg

grilled roasted pepper, ham and cheese sandwiches

For an uptown grilled cheese, try proscuitto in place of the ham and goat cheese in place of the Monterey Jack. **SERVES 2**

4 teaspoons softened butter, divided

4 slices whole-grain bread

4 thin slices (4 ounces) lean ham

1 bottled roasted red pepper, patted dry and thinly sliced

2 (1-ounce) slices Monterey Jack or Cheddar cheese

1. Spread 1 teaspoon butter on one side of each bread slice. Top unbuttered side of 2 bread slices with remaining ingredients, divided equally between the 2 slices. Place 1 bread slice on each sandwich (buttered side out).

2. Heat a large nonstick skillet over medium-low heat. Add sandwiches; cook until golden brown, about 5 minutes on each side.

PER SERVING: Calories 370; fat 19g; chol. 70mg; prot. 24g; carbs. 25g; fiber 4g; sodium 1240mg

muffaletta sandwich

A New Orleans classic. You'll have about 4 cups of olive mix, enough to make 3 sandwiches.

SERVES 8

NEW ORLEANS-STYLE OLIVE MIX:

2 cups chopped pitted green olives with pimientos (10-ounce jar, drained)

¾ cup chopped pitted kalamata olives

2 tablespoons finely chopped celery

¾ cup finely chopped carrots

½ cup finely chopped cauliflower

¼ cup chopped fresh flat-leaf parsley

½ cup finely chopped red bell pepper

2 tablespoons capers

¼ teaspoon celery seed

1½ teaspoons dried oregano

½ teaspoon dried rosemary

¾ teaspoon coarsely ground black pepper

1½ tablespoons white wine vinegar

¾ cup extra-virgin olive oil

SANDWICH:

1 loaf round Italian bread

1 to 1⅓ cups olive mix

4 ounces sliced mozzarella cheese

4 ounces sliced provolone cheese

4 ounces lean ham, thinly sliced

4 ounces hard salami, thinly sliced

4 ounces mortadella, thinly sliced (or any good-quality bologna)

1. To prepare olive mix, combine all ingredients in a large mixing bowl; stir well. Spoon mixture into a 1-quart jar with a lid. Refrigerate about 1 week before serving. (Keeps almost indefinitely in the refrigerator.)

2. To prepare sandwich, slice Italian bread in half lengthwise; spread 1 to 1⅓ cups olive mix on both halves. Layer cheeses and meats evenly on top. Place two halves of sandwich together; slice into wedges.

PER SERVING: Calories 370; fat 22g; chol. 45mg; prot. 20g; carbs. 24g; fiber 1g; sodium 1220mg

portobello and fontina panini

A panini maker is a great investment, but you can use a heavy skillet too. SERVES 2

2 round or oval crusty Italian sandwich rolls

1 tablespoon olive oil

2 large portobello caps (about 2 ounces each)

1 garlic clove, minced

1 tablespoon fresh or 1 teaspoon dried rosemary

¼ teaspoon salt

Coarsely ground black pepper

2 ounces fontina cheese, sliced

2 radicchio leaves, sliced

1. Preheat panini grill or stove-top griddle pan.

2. Cut rolls in half horizontally. Hollow out top and bottom halves of bread, leaving a 1-inch thick shell; reserve torn bread for another use. Brush cut sides of rolls lightly with oil.

3. Brush underside of mushrooms with oil. Place oil side down on panini grill or griddle. Grill 2 minutes or until bottom begins to brown. Turn mushrooms over; drizzle lightly with oil. Sprinkle with garlic, rosemary, salt and pepper. Grill about 4 minutes or until moisture collects in cap.

4. Place one mushroom, bottom side up on each roll bottom; top with cheese and radicchio. Cover with tops of rolls.

5. Place sandwiches on panini grill or griddle. Cover with grill top or grill press. Grill about 2 minutes on each side or until browned and cheese starts to melt.

PER SERVING: Calories 290; fat 17g; chol. 35mg; prot. 13g; carbs. 24g; fiber 2g; sodium 740mg

beef and black bean burgers

A happy marriage between an all-beef burger and a bean burger. SERVES 4

1 cup canned black beans, rinsed and drained

¾ pound lean ground beef

¼ cup diced red onion

1 teaspoon chili powder

½ teaspoon ground cumin

¼ teaspoon dried oregano leaves

½ teaspoon salt

Coarsely ground black pepper

4 hamburger buns

1. Prepare grill.

2. Place beans in a large bowl; mash with a potato masher. Add beef and remaining ingredients except buns; mix to combine. Divide meat mixture into 4 equal portions, shaping each into a patty.

3. Grill, broil or pan-fry until thoroughly cooked. Serve on hamburger buns.

PER SERVING: Calories 280; fat 6g; chol. 45mg; prot. 24g; carbs. 31g; fiber 5g; sodium 750mg

herbed buffalo burgers

Buffalo meat is very lean. We've added moisture by incorporating egg and cooked onion.

SERVES 6

BURGERS:

1 tablespoon olive oil

1 medium onion, finely chopped (about 1 cup)

1 garlic clove, minced

1½ pounds ground buffalo

1 teaspoon salt

½ teaspoon coarsely ground black pepper

½ teaspoon dried thyme, crushed

2 tablespoons chopped fresh parsley

1 egg

1 tablespoon Worcestershire sauce

TO ASSEMBLE:

Sharp Cheddar or American cheese slices

Hamburger buns

Lettuce, optional

Tomato slices, optional

Mayonnaise, optional

1. Heat olive oil in a medium skillet over medium heat. Add onion and garlic; sauté 5 minutes. Remove from heat.

2. Combine onion mixture and remaining burger ingredients. Divide meat mixture into 6 equal portions, shaping each into a ¾-inch-thick patty. Place on a tray lined with plastic wrap. Cover with more plastic wrap; refrigerate until ready to cook. (Patties may be prepared 1 day ahead).

3. Preheat grill. Place patties on grill rack over hot coals. Cook, covered, about 4 minutes. Turn burgers over, top with sliced cheese, cover and cook an additional 3 to 4 minutes or until done. Serve on hamburger buns with lettuce, tomato and mayonnaise, if desired.

PER BURGER (WITHOUT BUN AND TOPPINGS): Calories 360; fat 16g; chol. 100mg; prot. 28g; carbs. 24g; fiber 1g; sodium 820mg

for lower-fat burgers, *make your own with lean ground beef or turkey. Shape into individual patties and freeze. Take straight from freezer to grill.*

thai turkey burgers

There are times when we all need a new way to season ground turkey. Thai ingredients were the inspiration for this juicy burger. SERVES 4

**1 pound ground turkey
(not breast meat)**

4 green onions, minced

2 tablespoons minced fresh cilantro

2 teaspoons low-sodium soy sauce

**1 teaspoon minced
peeled fresh ginger**

Coarsely ground black pepper

4 hamburger buns

1.   Combine all ingredients except buns in a large bowl; mix gently. Divide meat mixture into 4 equal portions, shaping each into a patty.

2.   Grill, broil or pan-fry until thoroughly cooked. Serve on hamburger buns.

PER SERVING: Calories 330; fat 14g; chol. 90mg; prot. 25g; carbs. 23g; fiber 1g; sodium 570mg

black bean and rice burritos

This quick and easy burrito has it all—beans, rice, salsa and cheese. SERVES 6

1 (15½-ounce) can black beans, rinsed and drained

1 cup water

¾ cup instant whole-grain brown rice

⅔ cup, plus 6 tablespoons, salsa, divided

¾ cup (3 ounces) shredded sharp Cheddar cheese, divided

6 (10-inch) flour tortillas, heated

6 tablespoons sour cream

1. Combine beans, water and rice in a large saucepan; cover. Bring to a boil, reduce heat and simmer until rice is tender, about 10 minutes. Stir in ⅔ cup salsa. Remove from heat.

2. Sprinkle 2 tablespoons cheese down center of one tortilla. Top with about ½ cup rice mixture, 1 tablespoon salsa and 1 tablespoon sour cream; roll up burrito style. Repeat with remaining ingredients.

PER SERVING: Calories 410; fat 13g; chol. 24mg; prot. 16g; carbs. 57; fiber 6g; sodium 930mg

meatball calzone

This kid-pleasing meal can be assembled and frozen for up to 48 hours before baking. No need to thaw it. Just pop it in the oven. SERVES 6

Cooking spray

2 (10-ounce) cans refrigerated pizza crust dough (or Italian bread dough)

1 egg

1 tablespoon water

2 cups (8 ounces) shredded mozzarella and provolone cheese

1 (12-ounce) package pre-cooked frozen cocktail-size Italian meatballs (or regular size, cut in half)

1 (26-ounce) jar marinara or spicy Arrabiata sauce

1. Preheat oven to 400F. Coat a 14-inch round pizza pan with cooking spray.

2. Unroll dough onto work surface; pat into two 14-inch circles

3. Combine egg and water; brush dough in pan with some of the egg mixture. Sprinkle 1 cup cheese over dough and top with meatballs. Drizzle 1 cup of marinara sauce over meatballs; top with 1 cup cheese. Place remaining dough circle over pizza; pinch edges to seal. Brush dough with egg mixture. Cut several small slits in top of dough to allow steam to escape.

4. Bake 18 to 20 minutes or until top is golden and cheese bubbles. Serve with remaining sauce.

PER SERVING: Calories 660; fat 28g; chol. 65mg; prot. 33g; carbs. 69g; fiber 5g; sodium 1880mg

quick kids' pizzas

Next time a sleepover is in the works, be sure to let the kids create their own new tradition.

SERVES 4

½ cup chopped onion

1 garlic clove, minced

1 tablespoon olive oil

1 (8-ounce) can tomato sauce

1 teaspoon dried oregano

¼ teaspoon salt

¼ teaspoon coarsely
ground black pepper

1 (13-ounce) can refrigerated
pizza crust dough

½ cup (2 ounces)
shredded mozzarella

2 ounces small pepperoni slices

1. Preheat oven to 400F.

2. Combine onion, garlic and oil in a 4-cup glass measure. Microwave at HIGH 30 to 40 seconds. Add tomato sauce and oregano. Microwave at HIGH 2½ minutes; stir in salt and pepper.

3. Divide dough into 4 pieces. Press each piece into a 6-inch circle on a large baking sheet. Spread sauce over dough; sprinkle with mozzarella and top with pepperoni. Bake 10 minutes or until bubbling. Remove pizzas to cutting board; cut in wedges.

PER SERVING: Calories 360; fat 17g; chol. 20mg; prot. 14g; carbs. 45g; fiber 2g; sodium 1100mg

macaroni and cheese

pastas

pasta with bolognese sauce

Use a flavorful ham for the best results. Country ham, which is cured and smoked, is ideal here, but any flavorful ham or prosciutto works. **SERVES 6**

2 tablespoons butter

1 cup chopped onion
(about 4 ounces)

½ cup chopped carrot
(about 3 ounces)

1 pound ground pork

4 ounces minced country ham

1 cup dry white wine

1 (28-ounce) can crushed
tomatoes, undrained

½ teaspoon salt

½ teaspoon pepper

½ cup whole milk

2 garlic cloves, crushed

½ cup chopped fresh parsley

6 cups hot cooked fusilli or
other short twisted pasta

Melt butter in a large skillet over medium-high heat. Add onion and carrot; sauté until tender. Add pork and ham; cook 5 minutes. Add wine and cook until absorbed. Add tomatoes, salt and pepper; reduce heat and simmer, covered, 1 hour. Add milk, garlic and parsley; cook 15 minutes longer. Serve over pasta.

PER SERVING: Calories 570; fat 23g; chol. 75mg; prot. 27g; carbs. 55g; fiber 5g; sodium 700mg

linguine with cilantro pesto

Although basil is certainly the most common kind of pesto, this no-cook summer sauce can be made with a wide variety of herbs, including cilantro. Try it on chicken, fish and vegetables or as a dip. SERVES 6

3 garlic cloves

¾ cup fresh cilantro

½ cup fresh parsley

½ cup extra-virgin olive oil

⅓ cup (1½ ounces) finely grated Parmigiano-Reggiano cheese

¼ cup chopped walnuts (about 2 ounces)

1 tablespoon lemon juice

½ teaspoon kosher salt

½ teaspoon coarsely ground black pepper

6 cups hot cooked linguine (about 12 ounces uncooked pasta)

Place garlic in a food processor; pulse to chop. Add remaining ingredients except linguine; process until a paste forms. Toss pesto with warm pasta.

PER SERVING: Calories 430; fat 25g; chol. 5mg; prot. 10g; carbs. 43g; fiber 3g; sodium 230mg

penne with spinach, olives and sun-dried tomatoes

This simple dish incorporates handfuls of fresh spinach, convenient when you have a big bag of greens to use. It can be made with linguine or spaghetti as well. SERVES 6

1 garlic clove, finely chopped

½ teaspoon crushed red pepper

¼ cup extra-virgin olive oil

1 pound uncooked penne

2 (6-ounce) bags baby spinach, washed, trimmed and roughly chopped

½ cup pitted kalamata olives, roughly chopped

½ cup oil-packed sun-dried tomatoes, drained and roughly chopped

½ teaspoon salt

¼ cup (1 ounce) grated Parmigiano-Reggiano cheese

1. Combine first 3 ingredients in a large serving bowl; stirring with a whisk until well blended.

2. Cook pasta according to package directions, omitting salt and fat.

3. Add warm pasta and spinach to oil mixture. Toss until spinach wilts slightly. Add olives, sun-dried tomatoes and salt; toss well. Sprinkle with cheese.

PER SERVING: Calories 430; fat 13g; chol. 5mg; prot. 13g; carbs. 64g; fiber 5g; sodium 530mg

skillet ravioli and vegetables

No need to pre-boil refrigerated ravioli—simply sauté and steam briefly in a skillet. SERVES 6

4 tablespoons olive oil, divided

2 cups cauliflower florets (about 10 ounces)

1½ cups chopped bell peppers (red, green and yellow) (about 6 ounces)

1½ cups sliced mushrooms

3 garlic cloves, minced

1 cup low-sodium chicken broth, divided

2 (9-ounce) packages fresh vegetable or cheese ravioli

1 teaspoon dried Italian seasoning

1 cup dry white wine

½ cup (2 ounces) shredded Parmesan-Asiago-Romano cheese blend

¼ teaspoon salt

¼ teaspoon crushed red pepper

¼ teaspoon coarsely ground black pepper

1. Heat 2 tablespoons oil in a large skillet over high heat. Add cauliflower, peppers, mushrooms and garlic; stir. Cover and cook until browned, about 5 minutes, stirring occasionally. Remove vegetables. Add ¼ cup chicken broth to pan. Scrape pan to loosen browned bits; pour over vegetables.

2. Heat 2 tablespoons oil in the skillet over high heat. Add ravioli and Italian seasoning; cook, stirring until ravioli browns, about 2 minutes. Add wine and ¾ cup chicken broth. Reduce heat to medium and cook, covered until ravioli is tender and plump, about 3 minutes. Add reserved vegetables and remaining ingredients; cook until thoroughly heated, about 1 minute.

PER SERVING: Calories 290; fat 16g; chol. 20mg; prot. 10g; carbs. 21g; fiber 3g; sodium 520mg

macaroni and cheese

A combination of cheeses makes this the perfect mac and cheese: Cream cheese makes it creamy; Gruyère makes it sweet and nutty; Cheddar makes it sharp; and Parmigiano-Reggiano makes it salty and pungent. SERVES 8

Cooking spray

3 cups uncooked penne

1 egg

2 garlic cloves, minced

1½ cups 2% reduced-fat milk

1 cup (4 ounces) shredded sharp Cheddar cheese

½ (8-ounce) block cream cheese

1 cup (4 ounces) shredded Gruyère or Swiss cheese

¾ cup (3 ounces) grated Parmigiano-Reggiano cheese

⅛ teaspoon salt

⅛ teaspoon crushed red pepper

⅛ teaspoon black pepper

3 tablespoons butter

12 saltine crackers, crushed

1. Cook pasta according to package directions, omitting salt and fat.

2. Preheat oven to 350F. Lightly coat a 13 x 9-inch or 8-cup casserole dish with cooking spray.

3. Combine egg, garlic and milk in a medium bowl; mix well. Place pasta in prepared pan. Add milk mixture and remaining ingredients except butter and crackers; mix well.

4. Combine butter and crackers; sprinkle over pasta. Bake 30 minutes or until browned and bubbly.

PER SERVING: Calories 400; fat 23g; chol. 95mg; prot. 18g; carbs. 28g; fiber 1g; sodium 460mg

lasagna with cheddar cheese

Try this style of lasagna with a Cheddar cheese sauce and no ricotta layer for a unique break from the norm. **SERVES 12**

MEAT SAUCE:

1 pound lean ground beef

½ pound Italian sausage

1 cup chopped onion (4 ounces)

1 tablespoon minced garlic

1 cup dry white wine

2 tablespoons tomato paste

2 tablespoons chopped fresh parsley

½ teaspoon crushed red pepper

1 (15-ounce) can crushed tomatoes in purée, undrained

BÉCHAMEL SAUCE:

¼ cup butter

¼ cup all-purpose flour

½ teaspoon salt

¼ teaspoon pepper

¼ teaspoon ground nutmeg

3 cups 2% reduced-fat milk

Cooking spray

12 no-boil lasagna noodles

3 cups (12 ounces) shredded aged Cheddar cheese

1. To prepare meat sauce, cook beef and sausage in a large skillet over medium-high heat until browned; stir to crumble. Drain; return meat mixture to pan. Reduce heat to medium. Add onion and garlic; sauté 5 minutes. Add wine and bring to a boil. Reduce heat and cook, stirring occasionally, until wine is nearly evaporated. Stir in tomato paste, parsley and crushed red pepper. Add crushed tomatoes. Bring to a simmer over medium heat; reduce heat and simmer until sauce thickens, 10 to 15 minutes.

2. To prepare béchamel sauce, melt butter in a medium saucepan over medium heat. Whisk in flour, salt, pepper and nutmeg. Cook, stirring, 1 minute. Gradually add milk and continue to cook until thick and bubbly, about 10 minutes, stirring constantly with a whisk. Cool 10 minutes.

3. Preheat oven to 400F.

4. Spread ¾ cup tomato mixture in bottom of a 13 x 9-inch baking dish coated with cooking spray. Arrange 4 noodles over tomato mixture, overlapping slightly. Top with one-third of remaining tomato mixture, one-third of béchamel sauce and 1 cup Cheddar cheese. Repeat layers twice, starting with noodles.

5. Bake, uncovered, 35 to 40 minutes, until browned and bubbly, covering loosely with foil during the last 10 minutes if top browns too much. Let stand 15 minutes before cutting.

PER SERVING: Calories 330; fat 16g; chol. 60mg; prot. 18g; carbs. 25g; fiber 2g; sodium 410mg

seafood lasagna

No-cook lasagna noodles make preparing lasagna easy. The pasta softens as it bakes; you'd never know the noodles went into the pan right out of the box. **SERVES 10**

3 tablespoons butter

8 ounces sliced mushrooms

2 medium leeks (white part only), thinly sliced

¼ cup all-purpose flour

2 cups 1% low-fat milk

1 cup half-and-half

¾ pound medium shrimp, peeled, deveined and cut in half lengthwise

¾ pound bay scallops (if scallops are large, cut in half), pat dry

¼ teaspoon ground nutmeg

½ teaspoon kosher salt

Coarsely ground black pepper

1 cup bottled tomato-basil pasta sauce

1 cup (4 ounces) grated Parmigiano-Reggiano

Cooking spray

9 no-boil lasagna noodles

1 cup (4 ounces) shredded part-skim mozzarella cheese

1. Melt butter in a large nonstick skillet over medium heat. Add mushrooms and leeks; sauté 5 minutes or until leeks are softened. Sprinkle with flour; stir to combine. Add milk and cream; increase heat to medium-high and cook, stirring occasionally, until mixture comes to a boil. Reduce heat and simmer 1 minute. Add shrimp and next 4 ingredients (shrimp through pepper); stir. Cook over low heat until shrimp are pink, about 3 minutes. Remove from heat; stir in tomato-basil sauce and Parmigiano-Reggiano.

2. Preheat oven to 400F.

3. Spread 1½ cups tomato mixture in bottom of a 13 x 9-inch baking dish coated with cooking spray. Arrange 3 noodles over tomato mixture; top with one-third of remaining tomato mixture. Repeat layers, ending with sauce.

4. Cover with foil and bake 25 minutes. Remove foil, sprinkle with mozzarella and bake until browned, about 15 minutes. Let stand 10 minutes before serving.

PER SERVING: Calories 470; fat 22g; chol. 140mg; prot. 39g; carbs. 28g; fiber 1g; sodium 990mg

winter vegetable lasagna

Today, lasagna has a broad meaning. Use your own imagination and create a new lasagna with your favorite ingredients. Use butternut squash and winter greens for an autumnal version of lasagna. Salty provolone contrasts with the sweet squash perfectly. **SERVES 10**

SAUCE:

2 tablespoons olive oil

1 onion, chopped (about 4 ounces)

3 garlic cloves, minced

1 (28-ounce) can stewed tomatoes, undrained

1 (6-ounce) can tomato paste

½ cup dry red wine

1 tablespoon red wine vinegar

¼ teaspoon crushed red pepper

1 (6-ounce) bag fresh spinach, chopped

LASAGNA:

1 (15-ounce) carton part-skim ricotta cheese

1 egg

2 cups (8 ounces) shredded provolone cheese, divided

1¼ cups mashed cooked butternut squash (1 medium squash)

Cooking spray

12 no-boil lasagna noodles

4 cups torn turnip greens, blanched

¾ cup (3 ounces) grated Parmigiano-Reggiano cheese

1. Preheat oven to 350F.

2. To prepare sauce, heat olive oil in a large skillet over medium heat. Add onion and garlic; sauté 5 minutes. Add remaining ingredients except spinach and continue cooking 5 minutes; add spinach.

3. To prepare lasagna, combine ricotta, egg, ½ cup provolone and squash in a medium bowl; stir well to combine.

4. Spoon a small amount of tomato sauce in bottom of a 13 x 9-inch baking dish coated with cooking spray. Layer 4 lasagna noodles, turnip greens, ¾ cup provolone, half of ricotta mixture and one-third of remaining tomato sauce. Top with 4 more lasagna noodles, half of remaining tomato sauce, ¾ cup provolone and remaining ricotta. Top with 4 more noodles, remaining tomato sauce and Parmesan cheese.

5. Cover with foil; bake 40 minutes. Remove foil and bake until top is browned, 5 to 10 minutes.

NOTE: To cook butternut squash, slice it in half and place cut sides down in a roasting pan. Add water up to 1-inch. Bake 45 minutes or until tender at 375F. Scoop out pulp and mash.

PER SERVING: Calories 370; fat 16g; chol. 60mg; prot. 20g; carbs. 37g; fiber 5g; sodium 570mg

chicken with 40 cloves of garlic

poultry

baked chicken with dates

Use dates instead of raisins or cranberries for a sweet accent even in savory dishes. Look for plump, juicy, unsweetened dates in the produce section of most markets. Serve with couscous and Parmesan cheese. SERVES 6

12 chicken thighs (about 4½ pounds), skinned

1 cup pitted dates, halved

1 cup sliced pitted green olives

2 tablespoons olive oil

2 tablespoons white wine vinegar

4 garlic cloves, minced

½ teaspoon salt

½ teaspoon coarsely ground black pepper

¼ cup dry white wine or dry vermouth

1 tablespoon honey

1. Combine all ingredients except wine and honey in a 13 x 9-inch baking dish. Cover and marinate in refrigerator at least 2 hours or overnight.

2. Preheat oven to 350F.

3. Toss chicken mixture. Pour wine over chicken in pan and drizzle with honey. Bake, uncovered, about 1½ hours or until browned and fragrant, basting often.

PER SERVING: Calories 480; fat 27g; chol. 115mg; prot. 33g; carbs. 26g; fiber 3g; sodium 490mg

deep south chicken and dumplings

These are classic Southern dumplings—wet and sticky, more like pasta than biscuits. Look for frozen dumplings in the freezer section of supermarkets. SERVES 4

3 (14-ounce) cans low-sodium chicken broth

1 pound frozen boneless, skinless chicken breasts

¼ teaspoon dried thyme

1 bay leaf

½ teaspoon coarsely ground black pepper

1 (12-ounce) package frozen dumplings (such as Mary B's Open Kettle Dumplings)

1 cup frozen green peas (optional)

1. Combine first 5 ingredients in a Dutch oven; bring to a boil. Add dumplings one at a time, stirring to prevent sticking. Reduce heat, cover and simmer 20 minutes, stirring occasionally with a heatproof rubber spatula. Remove chicken; cool and shred.

2. Continue to cook dumplings, uncovered, until very tender, about 25 minutes, stirring occasionally.

3. When dumplings are done, return chicken to pan along with peas, if desired; cook 1 minute. Serve immediately in shallow soup bowls. Dish will thicken as it stands.

PER SERVING: Calories 440; fat 22g; chol. 60mg; prot. 21g; carbs. 38g; fiber 2g; sodium 1570mg

chicken fettuccine with herb cheese

Garlic and herb cream cheese is mixed with a little of the pasta cooking water to create a creamy sauce. SERVES 4

2 (14-ounce) cans low-sodium chicken broth

8 ounces frozen boneless, skinless chicken breasts

8 ounces uncooked fettucine noodles, broken in half

1 (16-ounce bag) frozen broccoli and cauliflower florets

1 (6-ounce) package garlic and herb cream cheese (such as Rondele)

½ teaspoon salt

2 tablespoons grated Parmigiano-Reggiano cheese

2 tablespoons finely chopped green onions

Coarsely ground black pepper

1. Bring broth to a boil in a deep skillet or Dutch oven over high heat; add frozen chicken breasts. Return to a boil, reduce heat, cover and simmer 16 minutes.

2. Stir in pasta; simmer, covered, 8 minutes, stirring occasionally. Remove chicken, cool and shred.

3. Increase heat to high and bring pasta to a boil. Add frozen vegetables, return to a boil. Cover tightly, reduce heat, and simmer until vegetables are crisp-tender, about 5 minutes.

4. Drain pasta mixture, reserving ½ cup of the pasta cooking water. Return mixture to pan and place over medium heat. Add cream cheese, salt and reserved cooking water. Toss until cheese has melted. Add chicken; cook 2 minutes, stirring frequently, until thoroughly heated. Sprinkle with remaining ingredients.

PER SERVING: Calories 500; fat 20g; chol. 100mg; prot. 26g; carbs. 51g; fiber 5g; sodium 1190mg

chicken with 40 cloves of garlic

An abundance of garlic, yes. But as the garlic cooks, it softens and mellows and is perfect for spreading on French bread. This recipe is a take on James Beard's classic dish. We've added cherry tomatoes and substituted basil and mint for the traditional tarragon. Serve with butternut squash or sweet potatoes.   SERVES 6

2½ cups sliced leeks or onions

¼ cup chopped fresh basil

1¼ cups chopped fresh mint

4 chicken leg quarters

1 cup dry white wine

1½ teaspoons salt

¼ teaspoon pepper

40 unpeeled garlic cloves
(about 4 heads)

2 cups cherry tomatoes

Sprigs of basil

French bread (optional)

1.   Preheat oven to 375F.

2.   Combine leeks, basil and mint in a 4-quart casserole. Arrange chicken over leek mixture. Pour wine over chicken and sprinkle with salt, pepper and garlic. Cover casserole with aluminum foil and casserole lid. Bake 1 hour. Add cherry tomatoes and bake 1 hour longer. Garnish with basil sprigs and squeeze garlic cloves onto French bread, if desired.

PER SERVING: Calories 280; fat 11g; chol. 70mg; prot. 22g; carbs. 16g; fiber 2g; sodium 660mg

peach and ginger–glazed chicken

A mildly spicy golden glaze brushed over chicken quarters or breasts turns them into a juicy main course with a minimum of fuss. Double the glaze mixture and refrigerate half for a later use on salmon or shrimp. SERVES 4

⅔ cup peach preserves

2 tablespoons finely grated peeled fresh ginger

2 garlic cloves, crushed

2 tablespoons low-sodium soy sauce

1 tablespoon spiced tea (such as Constant Comment) or other black tea leaves

⅛ teaspoon crushed red pepper, optional

1 to 2 teaspoons vegetable oil

½ teaspoon salt

¼ teaspoon coarsely ground black pepper

4 chicken quarters, skinned

2 thinly sliced green onions

1. Preheat oven to 350F.

2. Place first 5 ingredients (preserves through tea) in a food processor; pulse until chunky. Scrape into a bowl; add red pepper flakes, if desired.

3. Heat oil in a large, heavy, ovenproof skillet over medium-high heat. Sprinkle salt and pepper over chicken; add to pan and brown well, 6 to 8 minutes. Pour glaze over chicken.

4. Transfer pan to oven and bake about 40 minutes, until chicken is thoroughly cooked and glaze has thickened, basting occasionally with sauce. Remove pan from oven and sprinkle green onions over chicken.

PER SERVING: Calories 350; fat 7g; chol. 90mg; prot. 35g; carbs. 36g; fiber 0g; sodium 560mg

lemon-herb chicken with yogurt-dill sauce

Perfect for outdoor summer parties or picnics, this dish is loaded with the flavor of fresh herbs. SERVES 6

YOGURT DILL SAUCE:

1½ cups plain fat-free yogurt

1 garlic clove, minced

2 tablespoons extra-virgin olive oil

2 tablespoons chopped fresh dill

1 tablespoon lemon juice

½ teaspoon salt

CHICKEN:

Cooking spray

1 cup chopped fresh basil

¼ cup chopped fresh mint

2 tablespoons chopped fresh dill

¼ cup extra-virgin olive oil

6 garlic cloves, minced

Grated rind of 1 lemon

Juice of 1 lemon

4 chicken breast halves
(about 2½ pounds)

4 chicken thighs (about 2 pounds)

1½ teaspoons salt

¼ teaspoon coarsely
ground black pepper

Lemon wedges

1. To prepare dill sauce, drain yogurt in a strainer lined with cheesecloth for 2 hours or overnight. Transfer yogurt to a bowl; stir in remaining ingredients.

2. Preheat oven to 450F.

3. To prepare chicken, place a large wire rack on a shallow baking sheet and coat with cooking spray. Place basil and next 6 ingredients (basil through lemon juice) in a large bowl; stir to combine. Add chicken; toss well to coat. Arrange chicken in a single layer on prepared pan; sprinkle with salt and pepper.

4. Bake chicken breasts 30 to 40 minutes, until an instant-read thermometer inserted into the thickest part of the breast registers 170F. Bake chicken thighs 35 to 45 minutes, until an instant-read thermometer inserted into the thickest part of the thigh registers 180F. Serve immediately with lemon wedges and yogurt mixture.

Per serving: Calories 340; fat 21g; chol. 95mg; prot. 32g; carbs. 5g; fiber 0g; sodium 660mg

grilled chicken with spinach, feta and red pepper sauce

This is a perfect late-summer dish when peppers are abundant and cheap and the grill still calls. **SERVES 4**

GRILLED CHICKEN:

4 boneless, skinless chicken breasts (about 1½ pounds)

3 tablespoons extra-virgin olive oil

4 teaspoons kosher salt

Coarsely ground black pepper

ROASTED RED PEPPER SAUCE:

2 red bell peppers (about 1 pound)

3 tablespoons extra-virgin olive oil

1 tablespoon balsamic vinegar

¼ teaspoon salt

Coarsely ground black pepper

1 cup (4 ounces) crumbled feta cheese

10 ounces spinach

1. To prepare chicken, place all ingredients in a large zip-top plastic bag; seal and marinate in refrigerator 2 to 24 hours.

2. Prepare grill.

3. To prepare sauce, place peppers on grill rack and cook, turning occasionally, until charred. Place in a paper or plastic zip-top bag to let steam 10 minutes. Peel and seed peppers.

4. Place peppers and remaining ingredients in a food processor; process until smooth.

5. Remove chicken from marinade; discard marinade. Place chicken on grill rack and cook, covered, 7 minutes. Turn, top with feta and cook another 7 minutes until thoroughly cooked.

6. Arrange spinach on serving platter, top with chicken and serve with red pepper sauce.

PER SERVING: Calories 380; fat 22g; chol. 100mg; prot. 33g; carbs. 12g; fiber 4g; sodium 1240mg

chicken in tomato-peanut sauce

The chicken and vegetables are sautéed before adding to the slow cooker, but you can skip these steps in you prefer. Serve over basmati rice. SERVES 6

6 boneless, skinless chicken thighs (about 2¼ pounds)

¼ cup dry breadcrumbs

2 tablespoons vegetable oil

1 cup diced onion

½ cup diced red bell pepper

1 (14½-ounce) can diced tomatoes, undrained

⅓ cup peanut butter

2 garlic cloves, crushed

2 tablespoons brown sugar

2 tablespoons low-sodium soy sauce

⅛ teaspoon crushed red pepper, or to taste

½ cup canned low-sodium chicken broth

3 tablespoons coarsely chopped dry-roasted peanuts

Chopped fresh cilantro

1. Dredge chicken in breadcrumbs. Heat oil in a large nonstick skillet over medium-high heat; add chicken and cook until golden brown on both sides. Transfer chicken to a 3½ to 4-quart slow cooker.

2. Add onion and bell pepper to skillet. Cook until onion is translucent, about 4 minutes, stirring frequently. Stir in tomatoes and next 6 ingredients (tomatoes through broth). Spoon tomato mixture over chicken in slow cooker.

3. Cover and cook on LOW 3 hours or until chicken is tender. Serve with peanuts and cilantro.

PER SERVING: Calories 350; fat 22g; chol. 50mg; prot. 22g; carbs. 18g; fiber 3g; sodium 850mg

braised chicken thighs with tomatoes and smoked paprika

Cooking the thighs slowly produces fall-off-the-bone chicken. Serve with white rice or corn tortillas. Look for smoked paprika next to the Hungarian paprika. SERVES 4

8 skinless chicken thighs (about 3 pounds)

1½ teaspoons kosher salt, divided

Coarsely ground black pepper

1 tablespoon olive oil

2 large sweet onions, thinly sliced (about 12 ounces)

2 large carrots, cut into ½-inch-thick pieces

2 garlic cloves, minced

2 bay leaves

¼ cup dry sherry

1 tablespoon smoked Spanish paprika

1½ teaspoons ground ancho chili powder

1 teaspoon dried Mexican oregano, crushed

¼ teaspoon ground red pepper

1 (28-ounce) can peeled tomatoes, undrained

1. Preheat oven to 325F.

2. Trim excess fat from chicken thighs and season with 1 teaspoon salt and black pepper.

3. Heat oil in a Dutch oven or deep ovenproof skillet over medium-high heat. Add half the chicken and cook until golden brown, 4 to 5 minutes on each side. Transfer to a plate. Repeat with remaining chicken. Add onions and carrots and ½ teaspoon salt to the pan; sauté about 6 minutes. Add garlic, bay leaves and sherry; cook 2 minutes, scraping pan to loosen browned bits. Add paprika, chili powder, oregano and ground red pepper; stir until vegetables are coated with spices.

4. Add tomatoes; cook 2 minutes, breaking up larger pieces. Return chicken to pan; cover and bake 2½ hours.

PER SERVING: Calories 290; fat 9g; chol. 115mg; prot. 30g; carbs. 21g; fiber 5g; sodium 1070mg

we love Spanish smoked paprika. *It's a great way to impart a subtle smokiness to any food.*

chicken tetrazzini with sherry

This classic is always a great use for leftover chicken or turkey.   SERVES 6

8 ounces uncooked spaghetti, broken in half

¼ cup butter

1 (8-ounce) package presliced mushrooms

⅓ cup all-purpose flour

1 (14½-ounce) can low-sodium chicken broth

1⅓ cups half-and-half

3 tablespoons dry sherry

¾ teaspoon kosher salt

⅛ teaspoon ground nutmeg

¼ teaspoon coarsely ground black pepper

3 cups chopped cooked chicken breast (about 1 pound)

½ cup (2 ounces) grated Parmigiano-Reggiano cheese

1. Heat oven to 425F.

2. Cook spaghetti according to package directions.

3. While spaghetti cooks, melt butter in a large nonstick skillet over medium-high heat. Add mushrooms; sauté until browned, about 4 minutes. Sprinkle with flour and stir to combine. Add broth and half-and-half. Cook until mixture comes to a boil, stirring frequently. Reduce heat; simmer 2 minutes, stirring constantly. Add sherry, salt, nutmeg and pepper; stir. Remove from heat; add chicken.

4. Combine spaghetti and chicken mixture; toss gently and spoon into a 13 x 9-inch baking dish or shallow 3-quart casserole; sprinkle with cheese. Bake 20 minutes or until golden brown and bubbly (not brown).

PER SERVING: Calories 430; fat 18g; chol. 90mg; prot. 28g; carbs. 39g; fiber 2g; sodium 1010mg

chicken pot pie

A good chicken pot pie is not complicated, but it does take some time to assemble. We've sidestepped the most time-consuming step by using refrigerated pie dough. SERVES 8

¼ cup butter

½ cup diced onion

½ cup diced celery

1 (8-ounce) package presliced mushrooms

⅓ cup all-purpose flour

1 (14½-ounce) can low-sodium chicken broth

1¼ cups 2% reduced-fat milk

3 cups chopped cooked chicken (about 1 pound)

1 cup frozen peas

⅓ cup chopped fresh parsley

¼ teaspoon dried thyme

½ teaspoon salt

¼ teaspoon coarsely ground black pepper

Cooking spray

½ (15-ounce) package refrigerated pie dough

1 large egg yolk

1 tablespoon water

1. Preheat oven to 375F.

2. Melt butter in a large nonstick skillet over medium-high heat. Add onion, celery and mushrooms; sauté 6 minutes. Sprinkle flour over vegetables. Cook 1 minute, stirring constantly. Add broth and milk. Bring to a boil, stirring often. Reduce heat and simmer 2 minutes, stirring constantly.

3. Remove from heat; stir in chicken and next 5 ingredients (chicken through pepper). Spoon into 13 x 9-inch baking dish or shallow 3-quart casserole dish coated with cooking spray.

4. On a lightly floured surface, roll pie dough to about 1-inch larger than baking dish. Place dough over chicken mixture in pan; fold edges under; press with a fork to seal edges. Combine egg yolk and water; stir with a fork until well blended. Cut several small slits into crust; brush with egg mixture. Bake 40 minutes or until golden brown.

PER SERVING: Calories 350; fat 18g; chol. 95mg; prot. 21g; carbs. 24g; fiber 1g; sodium 330mg

cornish hens with middle eastern mojo de ajo

Mojo is a Cuban marinade traditionally containing oil, garlic and sour oranges (we've used lemons instead). Look for zaatar and sumac in Middle Eastern markets. SERVES 4

¼ cup vegetable oil

¼ cup olive oil

1 cup garlic cloves, thinly sliced (about 3 heads)

1 jalapeño pepper, seeded and very thinly sliced

1 tablespoon zaatar

½ tablespoon sumac

¾ cup lemon juice (about 6 lemons)

¼ cup chopped fresh parsley

¼ teaspoon salt

¼ teaspoon coarsely ground black pepper

4 small Cornish hens

1. Heat oils in a medium saucepan over high heat. Add garlic and carefully shake the pan until garlic starts turning golden. Remove from heat and quickly add jalapeño, zaatar and sumac. Add lemon juice, parsley, salt and pepper; cool in pan.

2. Combine hens and garlic mixture in a large zip-top plastic bag; seal and marinate in refrigerator at least 12 but no more than 24 hours.

3. Preheat oven to 375F.

4. Place hens, with marinade, breast side up in a roasting pan or 13 x 9-inch baking dish; let stand at room temperature 15 minutes before placing in oven.

5. Bake 1 hour or until skin is golden and juices run clear, basting occasionally with the marinade. Serve with pan juices.

PER SERVING: Calories 340; fat 15g; chol. 215mg; prot. 48g; carbs. 25g; fiber 0g; sodium 310mg

to get the most juice from lemons and limes,
keep them at room temperature, then roll briefly on countertop with palm of hand to loosen juice from membranes.

pomegranate-glazed turkey

The sweet-tart glaze gives this turkey a beautiful ruby sheen. SERVES 12

TURKEY:

Cooking spray

1 (12- to 14-pound) fresh or frozen turkey, thawed

1 teaspoon salt

¼ teaspoon black pepper

GLAZE:

⅓ cup pomegranate juice

1 tablespoon cornstarch

¼ cup honey

2 tablespoons balsamic vinegar

⅛ teaspoon ground cardamom (optional)

1. Preheat oven to 375F. Place a wire rack inside a shallow roasting pan; coat with cooking spray.

2. To prepare turkey, remove and discard giblets and neck. Rinse with cold water; pat dry. Sprinkle evenly with salt and pepper.

3. Place turkey, breast side up, on the prepared pan. Bake 1½ hours; rotate pan and bake an additional 1 hour.

4. To prepare glaze, place half the pomegranate juice in a small saucepan, add cornstarch and stir with a whisk to dissolve. Add remaining juice, honey, vinegar and cardamom, if desired. Bring to a boil; cook 1 minute, stirring constantly.

5. Remove turkey from oven. Brush turkey with half the glaze; return to oven. Bake 10 minutes; brush turkey with remaining glaze and bake 10 minutes longer or until an instant-read thermometer registers 180F. Let turkey stand 10 minutes before carving.

PER SERVING: Calories 280; fat 11g; chol. 90mg; prot. 32g; carbs. 11g; fiber 0g; sodium 370mg

grilled shrimp with orange and habanero mojo

mussels provençal

shrimp and corn pudding

shrimp and grits

grilled shrimp with orange and habanero mojo

pesto shrimp with couscous

shrimp, sausage and quinoa jambalaya

bay scallop sauté

roasted halibut à la bruschetta

salmon in parchment paper

sicilian tilapia

red snapper with mango salsa

fish & seafood

mussels provençal

Serve this savory dish with French bread for soaking up the sauce. SERVES 2

2 tablespoons olive oil

½ cup finely chopped red onion

1 medium fennel bulb, trimmed and chopped

2 garlic cloves, minced

1 large chopped seeded tomato (about 6 ounces)

1½ teaspoons chopped fresh or ½ teaspoon dried rosemary

1 teaspoon fresh or ½ teaspoon dried thyme

¼ teaspoon salt

¼ teaspoon coarsely ground black pepper

¾ cup dry white wine or dry vermouth

2 pounds mussels, scrubbed and debearded

1. Heat oil in a large Dutch oven over medium heat. Add onion; sauté 3 minutes. Add fennel and garlic; sauté 3 minutes.

2. Add remaining ingredients except mussels; bring to a boil. Stir in mussels; simmer, covered, until shells open, about 5 minutes. Discard any mussels that do not open.

PER SERVING: Calories 420; fat 18g; chol. 50mg; prot. 23g; carbs. 26g; fiber 5g; sodium 850mg

shrimp and corn pudding

In the Carolina and Georgia Low Country, corn comes into season just as the region's tidal creeks and inlets are teeming with tiny but intensely sweet inlet shrimp. In this recipe, the two are combined in a flavorful (and sweet) main-dish pudding that kids will love. Perfect for brunch. Serve with a tangy green salad.   SERVES 4

4 to 6 ears corn

2 tablespoons butter

5 green onions, thinly sliced

2 tablespoons chopped fresh parsley

2 eggs, lightly beaten

½ cup half-and-half

½ teaspoon salt

Ground white pepper

Ground red pepper

Freshly grated nutmeg

1 pound small to medium shrimp, or large shrimp cut in half, peeled

¼ cup all-purpose flour

1. Cut kernels from ears of corn into a large bowl; scrape "milk" and remaining pulp from cobs using the dull side of a knife blade to measure about 3 cups.

2. Preheat oven to 350F.

3. Melt butter in a sauté pan over medium-high heat; add onion. Sauté until tender, about 2 minutes. Add parsley. Remove from heat, and add to corn.

4. Stir in eggs and half-and-half. Season with salt, peppers and a generous grating of nutmeg.

5. Place shrimp in a medium bowl, add flour; toss to coat. Shake off excess flour and fold shrimp into corn batter. Pour shrimp mixture into a lightly buttered 2-quart casserole. Bake about 1 hour, until set and lightly browned. Serve immediately.

PER SERVING: Calories 420; fat 14g; chol. 360mg; prot. 39g; carbs. 34g; fiber 8g; sodium 690mg

shrimp and grits

This version of a Low-Country favorite is perfect for brunch. Be sure to use stone-ground grits for best flavor and texture. **SERVES 4**

Cheese Grits (recipe below)

6 bacon slices, chopped

1 pound raw shrimp, peeled and deveined

2 cups sliced mushrooms

½ cup beer

1 cup chopped green onions

1 garlic clove, minced

1 tablespoon lemon juice

1 to 2 dashes hot pepper sauce (such as Tabasco)

2 tablespoons chopped fresh parsley

Coarsely ground black pepper

1. Prepare grits. Keep warm in a double boiler.

2. Heat a large skillet over medium-high heat. Add bacon and cook until almost crisp. Remove bacon from pan.

3. Add shrimp and mushrooms to drippings in pan; sauté until shrimp are done, about 4 minutes. Add beer, onions and garlic; cook 2 minutes. Add remaining ingredients.

4. Divide grits among 4 plates. Spoon shrimp mixture over grits; sprinkle with crumbled bacon.

PER SERVING (INCLUDING GRITS): Calories 420; fat 15g; chol. 215mg; prot. 37g; carbs. 31g; fiber 3g; sodium 830mg

cheese grits

1½ cups water

1½ cups 2% reduced-fat milk

¾ cup stone-ground grits

¾ cup (3 ounces) shredded sharp Cheddar cheese

3 tablespoons grated Parmigiano-Reggiano cheese

¼ teaspoon salt

Coarsely ground black pepper

⅛ teaspoon hot pepper sauce (such as Tabasco)

Bring water and milk to a boil in a large saucepan over high heat; stir in grits. Cook according to package directions; remove from heat. Stir in remaining ingredients. If grits become too thick, add ¼ to ⅓ cup milk.

grilled shrimp with orange and habanero mojo

Mojo is a vibrant, spicy Caribbean sauce that comes in many forms but typically contains chiles, garlic, oil and juice. Keep this versatile sauce on hand to baste or marinade seafood, chicken and steak. This can be served as an appetizer as well. SERVES 2 AS ENTREES OR SERVES 4 AS APPETIZERS

HABANERO MOJO:

½ cup orange juice

2 tablespoons extra-virgin olive oil, divided

1 tablespoon fresh or pickled habanero chile, seeded and chopped

2 garlic cloves, minced

2 tablespoons chopped fresh cilantro

1 tablespoon Dijon mustard

½ teaspoon salt

Coarsely ground black pepper

SHRIMP:

2 tablespoons olive oil

2 garlic cloves, minced

8 raw jumbo shrimp, peeled and deveined

4 wooden skewers, soaked in water 30 minutes

Cooking spray

1. To prepare mojo, combine all ingredients in a small bowl.

2. To prepare shrimp, combine olive oil and garlic. Thread 2 shrimp onto each skewer; brush both sides of shrimp with oil mixture.

3. Prepare grill. Place shrimp on hot grill rack coated with cooking spray; grill 2 minutes on each side, basting with remaining oil mixture. Drizzle Habanero Mojo over shrimp before serving.

PER ENTRÉE SERVING: Calories 320; fat 29g; chol. 145mg; prot. 6g; carbs. 8g; fiber 0g; sodium 770mg

to minimize the heat in chile peppers, *remove the seeds—that's where most of their heat comes from.*

pesto shrimp with couscous

Sun-dried-tomato pesto is used in this recipe, but the traditional basil pesto also works well.

SERVES 2

⅓ cup low-sodium chicken or vegetable broth, heated

½ cup uncooked couscous

½ cup chopped red bell pepper

½ cup thinly sliced onion

2 tablespoons olive oil

½ teaspoon salt

Coarsely ground black pepper

½ pound raw large shrimp, peeled and deveined

¼ cup bottled sun-dried tomato pesto

1. Preheat oven to 425F.

2. Pour broth over couscous; cover and let stand 5 minutes.

3. Combine couscous and next 5 ingredients (couscous through pepper) in a medium bowl; mix well.

4. Cut two (15-inch) squares of parchment paper. Fold each square in half. Cut into heart shapes; open each. Place couscous mixture near fold. Arrange shrimp in a single layer over couscous mixture; top with pesto. Fold and tightly seal the edges with narrow folds.

5. Place packets on a baking sheet; bake 15 minutes. Remove packets from oven and transfer to individual serving plates; cut packets open.

PER SERVING: Calories 420; fat 16g; chol. 175mg; prot. 29g; carbs. 41g; fiber 3g; sodium 940mg

shrimp, sausage and quinoa jambalaya

Quinoa (KEEN-wah) is a South American grain. It's high in protein and a great alternative to rice and couscous. You can find it next to the rice in the supermarket.   SERVES 8

4½ cups low-sodium chicken broth, divided

2 cups uncooked quinoa

1 tablespoon olive oil

½ pound smoked turkey kielbasa, cut into ¼-inch thick slices

1 large onion, chopped

1 red bell pepper, thinly sliced

4 garlic cloves, peeled and chopped

1 cup spicy-hot vegetable juice (such as spicy V-8 juice)

1 pound raw medium shrimp, peeled and deveined

1 cup frozen peas

1 cup grape tomatoes, halved

1.   Combine 4 cups chicken broth and quinoa in a medium saucepan. Bring to a boil, reduce heat to low and cook, covered, 15 minutes.

2.   Heat oil in a large nonstick skillet over medium-high heat. Add sausage, onion, pepper and garlic; sauté until vegetables are tender, about 10 minutes. Add ½ cup broth and vegetable juice; bring to simmer. Add shrimp; simmer until thoroughly cooked, about 5 minutes. Add peas, tomatoes and cooked quinoa; toss.

PER SERVING: Calories 320; fat 8g; chol. 130mg; prot. 26g; carbs. 38g; fiber 5g; sodium 550mg

the best of relish cookbook

bay scallop sauté

Serve with crusty French bread for dipping in the sauce. Because scallops contain a lot of water that gushes out as soon as they are hot, they need a lot of heat applied quickly. It's important to pat the scallops dry and get your pan (and the oil mixture) very hot—this ensures the scallops brown and not water out. Also, make sure the scallops aren't crowded in the skillet as that will cause them to steam. **SERVES 3**

1 tablespoon canola oil

2 tablespoons butter

1 pound bay scallops, patted dry

1 garlic clove, slivered

1 tablespoon lemon juice

2 tablespoons white wine

¼ teaspoon salt

Coarsely ground black pepper

Chopped fresh parsley (optional)

1. Heat oil and half the butter in a large heavy skillet over medium-high heat until mixture starts to brown.

2. Add half the scallops and cook without moving until seared, about 30 seconds. Flip and sear other side, about 30 seconds. Remove from pan. Add remaining scallops and butter to pan and cook. Return first batch to pan and remove pan from heat.

3. Add garlic, lemon juice and wine. Season with salt and pepper and sprinkle with parsley, if desired. Serve immediately.

PER ENTRÉE SERVING: Calories 370; fat 14g ; chol. 135mg; prot. 49g; carbs. 10g; fiber 0g; sodium 810mg

roasted halibut à la bruschetta

Here is a main dish bruschetta (broo-SKEH-tah)—garlicky toast topped with flakey halibut steaks and tomato relish. The anchovies "melt" into the tomatoes creating a rich, flavorful topping. SERVES 4

6 tablespoons olive oil, divided

1 pound grape tomatoes, halved

½ cup finely diced red onion

5 flat anchovies, canned in oil, drained

3 large garlic cloves, crushed, divided

½ teaspoon salt, divided

Coarsely ground black pepper

4 (6-ounce) fresh or frozen halibut steaks

4 (¾-inch thick) slices good crusty bread

½ cup julienned fresh basil leaves

1. Preheat oven to 450F.

2. Heat 3 tablespoons olive oil in a large skillet. Add tomatoes, onion, anchovies and 2 crushed garlic cloves; stir. Cook over high heat, stirring constantly, until thick, about 5 minutes. Add ¼ teaspoon salt and pepper. Keep warm.

3. Stir together 3 tablespoons olive oil, 1 crushed garlic clove and ¼ teaspoon salt. Brush fish with half the oil mixture. Place on a rimmed baking sheet. Bake 10 minutes, or until fish is opaque and flakes easily.

4. Brush both sides of bread slices with remaining oil mixture. Toast in oven until golden brown, about 3 minutes.

5. Place a bruschetta on each plate. Top with tomato mixture and fish. Sprinkle with basil.

PER SERVING: Calories 440; fat 26g; chol. 50mg; prot. 34g; carbs. 17g; fiber 2g; sodium 670mg

---

need lots of crushed garlic? *Place peeled garlic cloves in a plastic bag and crush with the bottom of a bottle to avoid garlicky hands and cutting board.*

salmon in parchment paper

Cooking in parchment captures all the yummy juices from the salmon and vegetables. Serve with rice, orzo or bread for soaking up the juices. SERVES 4

4 cups arugula or baby spinach

4 (6-ounce) skinless salmon fillets

¼ cup white wine

2 tablespoons lemon juice

½ cup garlic and herb spreadable cheese (such as Alouette)

1 cup thinly sliced mushrooms

1 lemon, thinly sliced

1. Preheat oven to 400F.

2. Cut four (15-inch) squares of parchment paper. Fold each square in half. Cut into heart shapes; open each. Place arugula near fold; arrange salmon fillets on top of arugula. Drizzle salmon with wine and lemon juice. Spread cheese over salmon; top with mushrooms and lemon slices. Fold paper; seal the edges with narrow folds. Place packets on a rimmed baking sheet and bake 20 minutes. Remove packets from oven and transfer to individual serving plates; cut packets open.

PER SERVING: Calories 360; fat 23g; chol. 115mg; prot. 31g; carbs. 5g; fiber 1g; sodium 230mg

sicilian tilapia

Caponata (kap-oh-NAH-tah) is made of eggplant, onions, tomatoes, anchovies, olives, pine nuts, capers and vinegar cooked in olive oil. It is served as a salad, side or relish and is sold in the ethnic section of major supermarkets. **SERVES 6**

2 tablespoons olive oil, divided

3 garlic cloves, minced

2 (8-ounce) jars caponata (eggplant relish)

1 cup low-sodium chicken broth

¼ cup raisins

2½ pounds tilapia or other white fish fillets

1 (7-ounce) bag baby spinach (about 7 cups)

1. Heat 1 tablespoon oil in a Dutch oven or large deep skillet over medium heat; add garlic and cook 1 minute. Add caponata, broth and raisins. Bring to a boil, reduce heat and simmer 5 minutes.

2. Add fish to pan, pressing lightly to submerge in sauce. Cover with spinach; drizzle with 1 tablespoon oil. Cover and cook until fish is opaque in the center, about 8 minutes.

PER SERVING: Calories 370; fat 14g; chol. 135mg; prot. 42g; carbs. 19g; fiber 6g; sodium 450mg

red snapper with mango salsa

Panko or Japanese breadcrumbs are coarser and crunchier than American breadcrumbs. They create a delicious crunchy crust and are sold in the Asian section of major supermarkets.

SERVES 4

MANGO SALSA:

Grated rind of 1 lime

Juice of 1 lime

2 tablespoons pineapple juice

1 tablespoon extra-virgin olive oil

2 large diced peeled ripe mangoes

1 teaspoon grated peeled fresh ginger

1 small jalapeño chile, seeded and diced

¼ cup diced red onion

1 tablespoon chopped fresh parsley or cilantro

½ teaspoon salt

Coarsely ground black pepper

¼ cup diced red bell pepper

MACADAMIA-CRUSTED FISH:

4 (6-ounce) fresh red snapper fillets (or other firm white fish)

½ teaspoon salt

½ cup macadamia nuts (about 2 ounces)

¾ cup panko crumbs

2 eggs

2 teaspoons water

½ cup all-purpose flour

1 tablespoon butter

1 tablespoon olive oil

1. To prepare salsa, combine first 4 ingredients in a medium bowl; stir with a whisk. Add remaining salsa ingredients; stir to combine.

2. To prepare fish, sprinkle fish with salt. Place macadamia nuts and panko in a food processor; process until nuts are finely ground. Place nut mixture in a shallow dish. Combine eggs and water in a shallow bowl; stir with a whisk until well blended. Place flour in a shallow dish. Dredge fish in flour, dip in egg mixture, then dredge in nut mixture, pressing crumbs gently into fish.

3. Melt butter and oil in a large skillet over medium-high heat. Add fish; reduce heat to medium and cook until golden brown and fish flakes easily when tested with a fork, about 2 minutes each side. Serve with salsa.

PER SERVING: Calories 620; fat 27g; chol. 175mg; prot. 44g; carbs. 49g; fiber 4g; sodium 900mg

to cut a mango, *cut on each side of the seed that runs vertically through the fruit. Then score each half, cutting to—but not through—the skin. Invert each half so it looks like a porcupine and cut the fruit off.*

smoky dry mole-rubbed pork tenderloin

beef and onions braised in beer

garlic and herb beef tenderloin

rosa di parma

peppered beef with fruit salsa

cincinnati chili

cider-braised pork loin with carrots and onions

smoky dry mole-rubbed pork tenderloin

apricot and lamb tagine

lamb shanks with sun-dried tomatoes and white beans

meat

beef and onions braised in beer

Sometimes you slow-cook a meal to bring all the comforts of home to the dinner table. This dish is perfect over mashed potatoes and steamed Brussels sprouts.   **SERVES 6**

2 pounds boneless chuck roast, trimmed and cut into cubes

3 tablespoons all-purpose flour

2 tablespoons vegetable oil

2 onions, thinly sliced (about 8 ounces)

2 garlic cloves, chopped

2 teaspoons salt

¼ teaspoon black pepper

3 parsnips, coarsely chopped

1 (14-ounce) can beef broth

1 (12-ounce) bottle full-flavored beer

3 tablespoons red wine vinegar

1½ tablespoons brown sugar

½ teaspoon dried thyme

1. Preheat oven to 350F.

2. Sprinkle beef with flour. Heat oil in a Dutch oven or deep ovenproof skillet over medium heat. Add beef and brown on all sides. Remove beef from pan. Add onion to pan and cook until lightly browned, stirring frequently. Stir in garlic, salt and pepper; cook 5 minutes.

3. Return beef to pan. Add remaining ingredients. Cover and bake 1½ hours or until beef is tender.

PER SERVING: Calories 350; fat 14g; chol. 80mg; prot. 31g; carbs. 19g; fiber 3g; sodium 1140mg

garlic and herb beef tenderloin

If you can't find fresh marjoram and oregano, substitute fresh parsley and add a pinch each of dried marjoram and oregano. Perfect for a holiday dinner. **SERVES 12**

1 cup fresh basil leaves

3 tablespoons fresh rosemary

3 tablespoons fresh marjoram

2 tablespoons fresh oregano

6 garlic cloves

3 tablespoons Dijon mustard

¼ teaspoon black pepper

⅓ cup extra-virgin olive oil

Cooking spray

4¼ pound beef tenderloin, trimmed and tied

1½ teaspoons salt

1. Combine first 7 ingredients in a food processor. With processor on, slowly add oil through food chute; process until herbs and garlic are very finely chopped. Rub herb mixture over tenderloin; cover and marinate in refrigerator 4 hours or up to 24 hours.

2. Preheat oven to 425F. Coat a rimmed baking sheet with cooking spray.

3. Transfer beef to the baking sheet; sprinkle with salt. Bake 25 to 30 minutes or until a thermometer inserted into the center registers 135F for medium rare. Remove from oven and let stand 10 minutes before slicing.

PER SERVING: Calories 230; fat 12g; chol. 85mg; prot. 31g; carbs. 1g; fiber 0g; sodium 420mg

rosa di parma (filled beef tenderloin)

Spinach is added to this traditional dish, which is served in Italy for special occasions. Served with its pan juices, it pairs perfectly with potatoes. Proscuitto is a seasoned, thinly sliced, salt-cured ham. Although it has a distinct flavor, you can use any thinly sliced ham in its place. The tenderloin is "butterflied" in this recipe, forming a flat surface on which to place the fillings. SERVES 8

2½ pound beef tenderloin

¼ cup extra-virgin olive oil

4 garlic cloves, minced

Coarsely ground black pepper

1 (3-ounce) package sliced prosciutto

1½ cups (6 ounces) grated Parmigiano-Reggiano cheese

2 cups packed baby spinach (about 4 ounces)

1 teaspoon kosher salt

1 teaspoon dried sage

1 teaspoon chopped fresh rosemary leaves

1 tablespoon butter

½ cup brandy

Rosemary sprigs

½ cup beef broth

1. Slice tenderloin lengthwise, cutting to, but not through, other side. Open halves, laying beef flat. Cut each half lengthwise in half again. Place plastic wrap over meat; pound to ¼-inch thickness using a meat mallet or rolling pin.

2. Stir olive oil and garlic together. Brush tenderloin with half the garlic oil and sprinkle with pepper.

3. Arrange prosciutto over entire surface of beef. Top with cheese and spinach leaves. Roll up tenderloin, jelly roll fashion, into a long slender roll. Secure at 2-inch intervals with twine.

4. Mix salt, sage and chopped rosemary; rub into outer surface of tenderloin. Combine remaining garlic oil and butter in a Dutch oven or deep skillet over medium heat. Add tenderloin, turning to brown all sides.

5. Add brandy and rosemary sprigs to pan, allow brandy to reduce slightly. Add beef broth. Continue to cook, turning and basting with pan juices about 30 minutes for rare (140F) or until desired degree of doneness. Let stand 10 minutes. Remove twine and cut into slices.

PER SERVING: Calories 370; fat 20g; chol. 100mg; prot. 38g; carbs. 4g; fiber 1g; sodium 850mg

peppered beef with fruit salsa

Jalapeño pepper jelly and Worcestershire sauce give flank steak a kick. Fresh pineapple provides a cooling, fruity contrast to the pepper salsa. **SERVES 4**

SALSA:

1 cup diced fresh pineapple or mango

½ cup diced red bell pepper

¼ cup diced red onion

2 tablespoons chopped fresh cilantro

2 teaspoons minced jalapeño pepper

2 tablespoons lime juice

½ teaspoon kosher salt

Coarsely ground black pepper

BEEF:

¼ cup jalapeño pepper jelly

2 teaspoons Worcestershire sauce

1 teaspoon olive oil

1¼ pounds beef flank steak, patted dry with paper towels

½ teaspoon salt

¼ teaspoon coarsely ground black pepper

1. To prepare salsa, stir together all ingredients; cover and set aside.

2. To prepare beef, melt jelly in a small saucepan over medium heat; stir in Worcestershire sauce.

3. Heat oil in a large, heavy skillet over medium-high heat until hot but not smoking. Season both sides of steak with salt and pepper. Place in pan and cook about 4 minutes per side, turning once, or until desired degree of doneness.

4. Reduce heat to low and spoon jelly glaze over steaks. Cook 1 minute longer, until thoroughly heated and steak is glazed. Place steaks on serving plates; spoon salsa over each steak before serving.

PER SERVING: Calories 360; fat 13g; chol. 65mg; prot. 40g; carbs. 21g; fiber 1g; sodium 690mg

cincinnati chili

If you go to the Queen City, be sure to order a "3-way"—chili over spaghetti topped with finely shredded cheese. Cincinnati Chili is known for its unique taste attributed to allspice and a touch of cocoa. **SERVES 4**

¾ **pound lean ground beef**

1½ **cups finely chopped onion, divided**

1 **garlic clove, minced**

1 **(15-ounce) can low-sodium tomato sauce**

1½ **cups water**

2 **teaspoons unsweetened cocoa**

1½ **teaspoons chili powder**

½ **teaspoon salt**

¼ **teaspoon ground cumin**

¼ **teaspoon ground allspice**

¼ **teaspoon ground cinnamon**

⅛ **teaspoon ground red pepper**

1½ **teaspoons cider vinegar**

3 **cups hot cooked spaghetti (about 6 ounces uncooked)**

1 **(15-ounce) can red kidney beans, heated**

½ **cup (2 ounces) shredded Cheddar cheese**

Oyster crackers

1.   Cook beef and 1 cup onion in a large nonstick skillet over medium-high heat until beef is browned; stir to crumble. Drain well; return meat mixture to pan. Add garlic and next 10 ingredients (garlic through vinegar). Bring to a simmer, reduce heat and simmer uncovered 1 hour, stirring occasionally. Add water, if necessary, for a thinner consistency.

2.   Spoon meat sauce over cooked spaghetti, top with beans, ½ cup onions and cheese. Serve with oyster crackers.

PER SERVING: Calories 550; fat 17g; chol. 90mg; prot. 41g; carbs. 59g; fiber 10g; sodium 1340mg

the best of relish cookbook

cider-braised pork loin with carrots and onions

This dish smacks of fall and is perfect with a side of mashed potatoes on cool nights. **SERVES 6**

1 tablespoon vegetable oil

1 (2-pound) boneless pork loin

2 onions, vertically sliced (8 ounces)

4 carrots, cut diagonally into ¼-inch slices (about 12 ounces)

2 celery stalks with leaves, sliced (about 1 cup)

2 garlic cloves, minced

1 teaspoon dried rubbed sage

1 teaspoon dried thyme

1 teaspoon kosher salt

¼ teaspoon coarsely ground black pepper

1 cup apple cider

1. Heat oil in a Dutch oven over medium-high heat. Add pork and cook until well-browned on all sides. Transfer pork to a plate. Add onion, carrots and celery to pan; cook over medium heat, stirring occasionally, until onion is tender, about 10 minutes. Add remaining ingredients except cider.

2. Return pork and any accumulated juices to Dutch oven; pour cider over pork. Cover and simmer, basting occasionally, 1¼ hours or until a thermometer registers 160F. Remove pork from pan; let stand 10 minutes. Slice pork and serve with vegetables and pan sauce.

PER SERVING: Calories 320; fat 13g; chol. 90mg; prot. 34g; carbs. 16g; fiber 3g; sodium 430mg

smoky dry mole-rubbed pork tenderloin

Here is a simplified dry version of mole (MOH-lay) sauce, the traditional Mexican sauce made with nuts, chiles and chocolate. You'll have enough spice mixture for a couple of meals; store extra in an airtight container. You can also use a grill pan to cook the pork indoors. **SERVES 4**

1 cup hardwood chips

2 tablespoons cumin seed

1 tablespoon fennel seed

1 tablespoon mustard seed

1 tablespoon onion powder

1 tablespoon dried Mexican oregano or marjoram

1 tablespoon salt

⅓ cup chili powder

2 tablespoons unsweetened cocoa

½ tablespoon coarsely ground black pepper

1 pound pork tenderloin

Cooking spray

1. Soak hardwood chips in a bowl of water.

2. Toast cumin, fennel and mustard seeds in a dry cast-iron skillet over medium-high heat until they begin to smoke, about 5 minutes.

3. Combine seeds and remaining ingredients (except pork), in a spice grinder, mortar and pestle, or food processor. Grind to a powder.

4. Coat pork with spice mixture; refrigerate at least 30 minutes.

5. Prepare charcoal grill. When coals have turned amber and become ashy on the outside, push them to one side. Remove hardwood chips from water and pile them on top of coals. Position grate on grill and heat until chips begin to smoke, about 10 minutes.

6. Place pork on grill rack coated with cooking spray; grill 3 minutes on each side. Move tenderloin to the side of the grill with no coals. Cover grill, and cook 5 to 10 minutes. Let rest 5 minutes before slicing.

PER SERVING: Calories 140; fat 5g; chol. 55mg; prot. 20g; carbs. 6g; fiber 3g; sodium 970mg

apricot and lamb tagine

Dried apricots add vitamin A to this slow-cooked Moroccan stew.   **SERVES 6**

3 tablespoons canola oil

2 large onions, thinly sliced (12 ounces)

2 pounds boneless leg of lamb, trimmed and cut into 1-inch pieces

1 teaspoon ground turmeric

1 teaspoon ground ginger

½ teaspoon ground coriander

½ teaspoon ground cinnamon

½ teaspoon salt

½ teaspoon coarsely ground black pepper

¼ teaspoon ground allspice

3 cups low-sodium chicken broth

1 (15-ounce) can chickpeas

1 cup dried apricots (about 6 ounces)

1 tablespoon honey

1.   Heat oil in a large skillet over medium heat; add onion and sauté 5 minutes.

2.   Add lamb; cook, stirring occasionally, until pieces are no longer pink, about 4 minutes.

3.   Transfer lamb mixture to slow cooker; add remaining ingredients; stir. Cover and cook on HIGH 4 hours or LOW 8 hours.

PER SERVING: Calories 380; fat 13g; chol. 85mg; prot. 32g; carbs. 34g; fiber 6g; sodium 670mg

lamb shanks with sun-dried tomatoes and white beans

Serve in pasta bowls over Parmesan polenta or mashed potatoes. **SERVES 6**

1 (32-ounce) can low-sodium beef broth

1 large fennel bulb, trimmed and chopped

1 small leek, white and pale green parts only, halved lengthwise, and thinly sliced

6 garlic cloves, thinly sliced

2 tablespoons Dijon mustard

2 teaspoons finely grated lemon rind

1 teaspoon salt

1 teaspoon coarsely ground black pepper

4 (12-ounce) lamb shanks

½ cup halved sun-dried tomatoes (not oil-packed)

2 (15-ounce) cans white beans, drained and rinsed

Sprig of rosemary or ½ teaspoon dried thyme

3 tablespoons lemon juice

1. Combine first 8 ingredients in a 6-quart slow cooker. Add shanks in two layers (some will not be covered by liquid); cover and cook on HIGH 4 hours.

2. Reverse shanks top to bottom; cover and cook 2 hours. Add sun-dried tomatoes, beans and rosemary. Cover and cook until shanks are fork-tender, about 1 hour.

3. Remove shanks. Skim fat from sauce; stir and add lemon juice. Remove meat from bones and return meat to cooker; keep warm until ready to serve, up to 2 hours.

PER SERVING: Calories 430; fat 17g; chol. 120mg; prot. 44g; carbs. 26g; fiber 6g; sodium 610mg

orzo veggies

vegetarian meals

orange-glazed tofu

In this hearty recipe, water-packed tofu is roasted and basted in a bath of sweet-salty-savory flavors. Serve as you would chicken or beef, with a side of rice and a vegetable. **SERVES 4**

Cooking spray

2 (14-ounce) packages extra-firm water-packed tofu, drained

1 large seedless navel orange

3 tablespoons rice wine vinegar

⅓ cup white or light miso (soybean paste)

½ cup low-sodium vegetable broth

½ cup orange juice

½ cup mirin (sweet rice wine) or sherry

2 garlic cloves

3 tablespoons creamy peanut butter

1 tablespoon tomato paste

Ground red pepper or hot pepper sauce, to taste

⅛ teaspoon salt

Coarsely ground black pepper

1. Preheat oven to 425F. Coat a 13 x 9-inch baking pan with cooking spray.

2. Cut each block of tofu into 4 slabs, each about the size and shape of a deck of cards. Place tofu in prepared pan.

3. Grate rind from orange; place in a food processor. Peel orange; discard white pith. Cut orange in half; discard seeds. Place orange and remaining ingredients in food processor; process until smooth. Pour orange sauce over tofu in pan.

4. Bake 35 minutes. Remove pan from oven, turn tofu slices over and baste with sauce from pan. Return to oven, bake 20 minutes or until tofu is golden brown and very little glaze remains in pan. Cool slightly. Scrape edges of the pan to loosen any browned bits; stir into remaining glaze in pan. Serve warm with glaze from pan drizzled over tofu slices.

PER SERVING: Calories 370; fat 19g; chol. 0mg; prot. 27g; carbs. 19g; fiber 4g; sodium 1160mg

broccoli tofu cheese enchiladas

Firm tofu is puréed to make a creamy filling that is combined with crumbled tofu and broccoli in these vegetarian enchiladas. You can find jarred enchilada sauce next to the salsas in the supermarket. **SERVES 4**

FILLING:

Cooking spray

1 tablespoon olive oil

½ large onion, coarsely chopped (about 3 ounces)

3 cups coarsely chopped broccoli

1 (14-ounce) package firm water-packed tofu

¼ cup (2 ounces) block-style Neufchatel or regular cream cheese

2 garlic cloves, peeled and quartered

1½ teaspoons chili powder

1 teaspoon salt

ENCHILADAS:

8 (8-inch) corn tortillas

2½ cups red or green taco sauce or enchilada sauce

1 cup (4 ounces) grated sharp Cheddar or Monterey Jack cheese

1. Preheat oven to 400F. Coat a 13 x 9-inch baking dish with cooking spray.

2. To prepare filling, heat oil in a large skillet. Add onion and broccoli; sauté 5 minutes.

3. Place half the tofu in a food processor; coarsely crumble the remaining tofu into a large bowl. Add cream cheese, garlic, chili powder and salt to processor; process until smooth. Add onion and broccoli mixture; pulse a few times until coarsely chopped.

4. Spoon mixture into bowl with crumbled tofu; stir well to combine.

5. To prepare enchiladas, spoon about ⅛ of filling down center of each tortilla. Roll up and place seam side down in prepared baking dish.

6. Pour enchilada sauce over tortillas; bake 15 to 20 minutes. Remove from oven; sprinkle with cheese. Increase oven temperature to 450F; bake 5 to 10 minutes longer, until cheese melts.

PER SERVING: Calories 400; fat 16g; chol. 25mg; prot. 18g; carbs. 47g; fiber 5g; sodium 1700mg

frittata with chard and whole-wheat spaghetti

From spring through late October, when chard is at its peak, an omelet with whole-wheat pasta makes a quick and delicious supper. Use your largest shallow skillet. Serve with a salad and crusty whole-grain bread. **SERVES 5**

1 pound Swiss chard, trimmed and coarsely chopped

5 eggs

⅓ cup 2% reduced-fat milk

3 tablespoons grated Parmigiano-Reggiano cheese

⅛ teaspoon ground nutmeg

¼ teaspoon salt

Coarsely ground black pepper

2 cups cooked whole-wheat spaghetti (4 ounces uncooked pasta)

1 tablespoon butter

1 cup (4 ounces) shredded provolone or mozzarella cheese

1.   Rinse Swiss chard with cold water and place in a large Dutch oven with water clinging to the leaves. Cover; cook over medium heat until tender, 5 minutes. Drain thoroughly. When cool enough to handle, press between paper towels until barely moist.

2.   Combine eggs and next 5 ingredients (eggs through pepper) in a large bowl; stir in spaghetti and chard.

3.   Melt butter in a large oven-proof skillet. Add egg mixture; cover, and cook over low heat until top is almost set, 10 to 13 minutes.

4.   Preheat broiler. Sprinkle frittata with provolone and broil 3 minutes, or until golden brown.

PER SERVING: Calories 300; fat 16g; chol. 240mg; prot. 20g; carbs. 22g; fiber 4g; sodium 680mg

mushroom and black-eyed pea ragout with parmesan polenta

A ragout (ra-GOO) is a thick stew of meats or, in this case, vegetables. It's great with the creamy Parmesan polenta, but also good with mashed potatoes or even grits. **SERVES 6**

3 tablespoons olive oil

1 large onion, vertically sliced (about 6 ounces)

¼ pound shiitake mushrooms, tough part of stems removed, thickly sliced

¼ pound sliced mixed mushrooms (such as cremini, baby bella and oyster mushrooms)

4 garlic cloves, crushed

2½ cups mushroom or vegetable broth

1 tablespoon tomato paste

½ cup red wine

2 (15-ounce) cans black-eyed peas, drained

½ teaspoon salt

Coarsely ground black pepper

¼ teaspoon honey

⅛ teaspoon hot pepper sauce (such as Tabasco)

1 bunch hearty greens (kale, turnip, mustard or chard) washed, thinly sliced and blanched

Parmesan polenta (see page 175)

Fresh shaved Parmigiano-Reggiano (optional)

1. Heat oil over medium heat in a large nonstick skillet. Add onion, mushrooms and garlic; sauté until onions are soft, about 5 minutes.

2. Add broth and next 7 ingredients (broth through hot pepper sauce); bring to boil. Reduce heat; cook until sauce thickens slightly, about 20 minutes. Stir in greens; cook until thoroughly heated.

3. Spoon Parmesan polenta (see facing page for recipe) into serving bowls. Top with ragout and garnish with Parmesan shavings, if desired.

PER SERVING: Calories 250; fat 8g; chol. 0mg; prot. 10g; carbs. 39g; fiber 8g; sodium 400mg

parmesan polenta

Baked in a pan in the oven, this no-fuss, no-stir polenta is perfect with almost any spicy stew, such as our mushroom and black-eyed pea ragout.   **SERVES 6**

Cooking spray

½ teaspoon salt

3½ cups water or mushroom or vegetable broth

1 cup coarse, stone-ground yellow cornmeal

1 tablespoon butter

1 tablespoon extra-virgin olive oil

⅛ teaspoon ground cayenne pepper

4 ounces grated Parmigiano-Reggiano cheese

Coarsely ground black pepper

¼ cup warm milk, optional

1.   Preheat oven to 350F. Coat a 13 x 9-inch baking dish with cooking spray.

2.   Combine salt, water and cornmeal in baking dish. Stir well. (The mixture will separate, with meal sinking to the bottom.) Bake, uncovered, 30 minutes.

3.   Remove from oven; stir well. Bake 10 minutes.

4.   Stir in butter, olive oil, cayenne pepper, Parmigiano-Reggiano and black pepper. Add milk to thin polenta if desired. Serve immediately with Mushroom and Black-Eyed Pea Ragout.

PER SERVING: Calories 190; fat 10g; chol. 20mg; prot. 9g, carbs. 16g, fiber 3g, sodium 510mg.

tomato phyllo pie

Ripe, juicy tomatoes are a must for this yummy tart. Served with a salad, this makes a great vegetarian meal. You can use any size phyllo sheets and adjust the toppings accordingly. This recipe uses 14 x 18-inch sheets. Roll the edges to make a 9 x 13-inch tart with a rim. **SERVES 6**

¼ cup butter, melted

2 garlic cloves, crushed

8 phyllo sheets

1 cup shredded mozzarella cheese

3 medium red and orange tomatoes, sliced

1 cup (4 ounces) crumbled feta cheese

⅓ cup chopped fresh basil

1. Preheat oven to 375F. Lightly grease a large baking sheet.

2. Combine butter and garlic in a small bowl. Place 1 phyllo sheet on pan; lightly brush with butter mixture. Working with 1 phyllo sheet at a time, brush remaining 7 phyllo sheets with butter mixture, placing one on top of the other. Place a sheet of plastic wrap over phyllo, pressing gently to seal sheets together; discard plastic wrap.

3. Sprinkle top phyllo sheet with mozzarella, leaving a 2½ inch border. Top with sliced tomatoes. Sprinkle with feta cheese and basil. Fold over edges of phyllo to cover 2 inches of cheese mixture. Bake 20 to 25 minutes, until phyllo is crisp and cheese is melted.

PER SERVING: Calories 260; fat 17g; chol. 45mg; prot. 11g; carbs. 18g; fiber 1g; sodium 510mg

never put tomatoes in the refrigerator. *Cold temperatures turn them mealy and mute their flavor.*

orzo veggies

A great dish for your next potluck occasion. **SERVES 8**

1 pound asparagus, trimmed

1 medium red bell pepper

1 medium green bell pepper

1 medium yellow bell pepper

6 green onions, chopped

1 medium zucchini

1 cup grape tomatoes

4 tablespoons olive oil, divided

1 garlic clove, crushed

1 tablespoon Italian seasoning

¾ teaspoon salt

⅛ teaspoon coarsely ground black pepper

1 cup uncooked orzo (rice-shaped pasta)

2 cups low-sodium vegetable broth

½ cup toasted pine nuts, toasted (optional)

¾ cup (3 ounces) crumbled feta cheese

1. Preheat oven to 350F.

2. Cut first 7 ingredients into bite-sized pieces; place in a 13 x 9-inch baking dish. Add 2 tablespoons oil and next 4 ingredients (oil through black pepper); stir well to coat. Bake 30 minutes or until tender.

3. Place 2 tablespoons oil in a large saucepan over medium-high heat. Add orzo and cook until brown. Add broth; bring to a boil. Cover, reduce heat, and simmer until liquid is absorbed.

4. Add orzo to baking dish with roasted vegetables; stir to combine. Sprinkle with pine nuts, if desired, and cheese. Bake 30 minutes. Serve hot or at room temperature.

PER SERVING: Calories 310; fat 17 g; chol. 15mg; prot. 9g; carbs. 31g; fiber 4g; sodium 520mg

south texas vegetable tacos with goat cheese

If you have any vegetables left over, add them to scrambled eggs and serve in tortillas for breakfast. **SERVES 4**

2 poblano chiles, cut in half

2 tablespoons olive oil

1 large red onion, thinly sliced (about 6 ounces)

4 small zucchini, halved lengthwise and sliced (about 3 cups)

½ teaspoon kosher salt

1 cup fresh corn kernels

2 teaspoons dried oregano

½ cup chopped fresh cilantro

2 tablespoons fresh lime juice

Coarsely ground black pepper

1 cup (8 ounces) goat cheese

8 (8-inch) corn tortillas

1. Place poblano chiles on a foil-lined baking sheet; broil 3 inches from heat 8 minutes or until blackened, turning after 6 minutes. Place in a zip-top plastic bag; seal. Let stand 15 minutes. Peel chiles; cut in half lengthwise. Discard seeds and membranes. Chop each roasted chile.

2. Heat oil in a large skillet over medium-high heat. Add onion, zucchini and salt; sauté until lightly browned, about 7 minutes. Add corn; cook 2 minutes. Add oregano, cilantro, lime juice and chiles; cook until thoroughly heated, stirring constantly. Season with black pepper.

3. Heat tortillas according to package directions. Spread 2 tablespoons goat cheese onto each tortilla. Top with vegetable mixture and serve immediately.

PER SERVING: Calories 480; fat 27g; chol. 45mg; prot. 17g; carbs. 45g; fiber 6g; sodium 610mg

african peanut stew

This popular African dish is usually prepared with chicken, but using edamame makes it super-nutritious. In addition, the tomatoes, sweet potatoes and spinach infuse it with fiber, protein and antioxidants. Serve on rice for a hearty main dish. **SERVES 8**

1 tablespoon olive oil

1½ cup finely chopped red onion (about 2 medium)

1¼ cups finely chopped green bell pepper (about 1 large)

½ cup chopped carrot (1 medium)

½ cup chopped celery (about 2 medium stalks)

3 garlic cloves, minced

2 tablespoons minced peeled fresh ginger

1 tablespoon curry powder

1 (14½-ounce) can diced tomatoes, drained

1 bay leaf

4 cups fat-free, low-sodium vegetable broth

1 large sweet potato, peeled and cut into ½-inch pieces (about 12 ounces)

1½ cups shelled edamame

¼ cup creamy or crunchy natural peanut butter or almond butter

¼ cup chopped fresh cilantro

1 (6-ounce) bag baby spinach, torn into bite-size pieces

½ teaspoon salt

Coarsely ground black pepper

1. Heat oil in a 4-quart saucepan or Dutch oven over medium heat. Add onion and next 3 ingredients (onion through celery); sauté until soft and translucent, about 5 minutes.

2. Add garlic, ginger and curry powder, sauté until fragrant, about 1 minute (do not brown garlic). Add tomatoes and bay leaf; cook, uncovered, until tomatoes are slightly reduced, about 3 minutes.

3. Add broth and sweet potatoes; bring to a boil. Reduce heat and simmer about 8 minutes. Add edamame and peanut butter; stir to combine. Cook until thoroughly heated, about 2 minutes. Stir in cilantro and spinach; cook until spinach wilts. Season with salt and pepper.

PER SERVING: Calories 190; fat 8g; chol. 0mg; prot. 11g; carbs. 21g; fiber 5g; sodium 570mg

---

edamame *(young green soybeans) are a great nutritious stand-in for almost any dried bean in any recipe.*

cherry plum cobbler

rustic apple pie

dried apricot pie

blackberry slump

banana cream pie

fresh cherry tart

cherry plum cobbler

date nut tart

orange meringue pie

pear streusel pie

crusty rhubarb pie

chocolate cake with peanut butter frosting

flourless chocolate cake with strawberries and cream

coconut crumb cake

honey cheesecake

pumpkin cupcakes with maple cream cheese icing

chocolate relish bars

thyme angel food cake

almond butter oatmeal cookies

molasses cookies

gluten-free chocolate chip cookies

two cranberry ice cream

desserts

rustic apple pie

This substantial apple pie is made in a tall springform pan, giving a new meaning to "deep-dish." SERVES 12

CRUST:

2½ cups all-purpose flour

1 teaspoon salt

¾ cup vegetable shortening

6 to 7 tablespoons ice water

FILLING:

11 cups sliced peeled Granny Smith apples (about 4 pounds)

½ cup all-purpose flour

1½ cups granulated sugar

1 teaspoon ground cinnamon

½ teaspoon salt

3 tablespoons butter, cut into small pieces

Cinnamon-sugar (optional)

1. Preheat oven to 375F.

2. To prepare crust, combine flour and salt in a large bowl; cut in shortening with a pastry blender or two knives until mixture resembles coarse meal. Sprinkle surface with ice water, 1 tablespoon at a time; tossing with a fork until moist and crumbly.

3. Press two-thirds of mixture into a disk on plastic wrap; cover. Press remaining mixture into a disk on plastic wrap; cover. Chill both disks for 15 minutes. Roll out larger disk on a lightly floured surface until large enough to cover the bottom and side of a 9-inch springform pan, with about 2 inches of overhang. Roll out small disk into a 9-inch circle. Place larger circle into pan.

4. To prepare filling, combine apples and next 4 ingredients (apples through salt); toss well. Spoon filling into crust. Arrange butter on top. Place top crust over filling; fold overhang evenly over top crust. Cut 10 to 12 slits in top crust; sprinkle with cinnamon-sugar, if desired. Bake 1 hour or until filling is bubbly and crust is deep golden.

PER SERVING: Calories 440; fat 18g; chol. 10mg; prot. 4g; carbs. 71g; fiber 4g; sodium 380mg

dried apricot pie

A great winter fruit pie that can be enjoyed all year long. SERVES 12

3 cups chopped dried apricots

**1 (6-ounce) package
dried cranberries**

½ cup golden raisins

1 egg, beaten

1 egg yolk, beaten

1 cup packed dark brown sugar

½ cup coarsely ground walnuts

**½ cup unsalted butter,
melted and cooled**

2 teaspoons vanilla extract

½ teaspoon ground cinnamon

¼ teaspoon salt

**1 (15-ounce) package refrigerated
pie dough (such as Pillsbury)**

1. Combine first 3 ingredients a large saucepan. Cover with water to 2 inches above fruit; bring to a boil, reduce heat and simmer 5 minutes. Drain. Cool 15 minutes.

2. Preheat oven to 350F.

3. Place egg and next 7 ingredients (egg through salt) in a large bowl; stir until well blended. Add fruit mixture; stir to combine.

4. Place 1 sheet of pie dough into a 9-inch pie plate, allowing dough to extend over edge of dish. Spread filling evenly into crust. Cut second crust into strips; form lattice over pie filling. Fold edges under; flute.

5. Bake 1 hour or until filling is bubbly and crust is browned. Cool on a wire rack at least 1 hour before serving.

Per serving: Calories 410; fat 20g; chol. 65mg; prot. 4g; carbs. 55g; fiber 6g; sodium 210mg

blackberry slump

A slump is an old-fashioned New England dessert of fruit, usually berries, topped with biscuit dough and baked. **SERVES 6**

3 pints ripe blackberries

¾ cup sugar, divided

2 cups, plus 1 tablespoon, all-purpose flour

1 grated lemon rind

1 tablespoon lemon juice

6 tablespoons cold unsalted butter, cut into small pieces, divided

2 tablespoons bourbon (or 1 teaspoon vanilla extract)

1 teaspoon ground cinnamon

¾ teaspoon salt, divided

2 teaspoons baking powder

½ teaspoon baking soda

1 cup buttermilk

1. Preheat oven to 375F.

2. Combine berries, ½ cup sugar and 1 tablespoon flour in a large bowl; toss gently. Add lemon rind and juice, 3 tablespoons butter, bourbon, cinnamon and ¼ teaspoon salt; toss gently. Spoon fruit mixture into a greased 2-quart casserole dish.

3. Combine 2 cups flour, ¼ cup sugar, ½ teaspoon salt, baking powder and baking soda. Cut in 3 tablespoons butter with a pastry blender or two knives until mixture resembles coarse meal. Add buttermilk; stir just until moist. Drop dough by large spoonfuls onto blackberry mixture.

4. Place pan on a rimmed baking sheet. Bake 45 to 50 minutes, until filling is bubbly and crust is browned.

PER SERVING: Calories 340; fat 13g; chol. 35mg; prot. 8g; carbs. 47g; fiber 8g; sodium 620mg

banana cream pie

Use bananas that are firm but ripe. To decrease the fat in this pie, serve with fat-free whipped topping in place of the whipped cream. SERVES 8

GRAHAM CRACKER CRUST:

18 graham crackers

¼ cup granulated sugar

1 teaspoon ground cinnamon

1 tablespoon butter, melted

1 egg white

Cooking spray

FILLING:

¾ cup granulated sugar

¼ cup cornstarch

¼ teaspoon salt

4 egg yolks

2¼ cups whole milk, divided

3 tablespoons unsalted butter

2 teaspoons vanilla extract

3 bananas, sliced (about 1 pound)

TOPPING:

1 cup whipping cream

2 tablespoons powdered sugar

½ teaspoon vanilla extract

1. Preheat oven to 325F.

2. To prepare crust, place crackers in a food processor and process until finely ground. Add sugar, cinnamon and butter; process 10 to 15 seconds. Add egg white and pulse 10 times or until crumbs are moist. Press crumbs firmly into bottom and up sides of a 9-inch pie plate coated with cooking spray; bake 15 minutes or until light brown and fragrant. Cool completely on a wire rack.

3. To prepare filling, whisk together granulated sugar, cornstarch and salt in a heavy medium saucepan. Add egg yolks and ½ cup milk; whisk until smooth. Place 1¾ cups milk in a microwave-safe bowl; microwave on HIGH until very hot, about 2 minutes. Whisk hot milk into sugar mixture in pan; cook over medium heat until thick and boiling. Continue cooking, stirring constantly 1 minute; remove from heat. Stir in butter and vanilla. Cool to room temperature; stir occasionally.

4. Spread about ½ cup cooled filling into crust. Arrange sliced bananas evenly over filling; spoon remaining filling over bananas. Refrigerate 3 to 4 hours.

5. To prepare topping, just before serving, combine cream, powdered sugar and vanilla in a medium bowl; beat with a mixer at high speed until stiff peaks form. Spread evenly over pie.

PER SERVING: Calories 420; fat 23g; chol. 170mg; prot. 6g; carbs. 50g; fiber 2g; sodium 220mg

fresh cherry tart

Chilling the pastry dough before rolling helps prevent shrinking when it bakes. **SERVES 8**

PASTRY:

1¼ cups all-purpose flour

2 tablespoons granulated sugar

¼ teaspoon salt

½ cup butter, chilled and cut into small pieces

2 teaspoons grated orange rind

1 to 2 teaspoons ice water

CHERRY FILLING:

4 cups pitted cherries (about 1⅓ pounds)

⅔ cup granulated sugar

1½ tablespoons cornstarch

1 teaspoon powdered sugar

1. To prepare pastry, place first 3 ingredients in a food processor; pulse 2 times or until combined. Add butter and orange rind; pulse 4 times or until mixture resembles coarse meal. With processor on, add ice water through food chute, processing just until combined.

2. Press mixture gently into a 4-inch disk on plastic wrap; cover. Chill 15 minutes. Roll dough on a lightly floured surface into a 15-inch circle. Place in a 10-inch tart pan with removable bottom, letting pastry hang over edge. Press dough against sides of pan.

3. Preheat oven to 375F.

4. To prepare filling, combine cherries, granulated sugar and cornstarch. Spoon mixture into prepared tart pan; fold edges of dough over filling.

5. Bake 40 minutes or until filling is bubbly and crust is browned. Cool on wire rack. Sift powdered sugar over pastry before serving.

PER SERVING: Calories 270; fat 11g; chol. 30; prot. 3g; carbs. 42g; fiber 2g; sodium 75mg

keep butter cold *when making a streusel mixture or pie pastry. Cold butter creates a flaky crust.*

cherry plum cobbler

Fresh cherries and plums make a delicious combo in this comforting summer dessert. SERVES 9

BISCUITS:

1¼ cups all-purpose flour

¼ cup sugar

2 teaspoons baking powder

¼ teaspoon salt

¼ cup vegetable shortening

⅓ cup buttermilk

FRUIT FILLING:

**4 cups pitted cherries
(about 1⅓ pounds)**

**3 cups sliced plums
(about 1¼ pounds)**

¾ cup sugar

1 tablespoon cornstarch

⅛ teaspoon ground nutmeg

¼ cup orange juice

1. To prepare biscuits, combine flour, sugar, baking powder and salt in a large bowl. Cut in shortening with a pastry blender or 2 knives until mixture resembles coarse meal. Add buttermilk; stirring just until moist.

2. Preheat oven to 375F.

3. To prepare fruit filling, combine all filling ingredients; mix gently. Spoon into a 1½-quart baking dish.

4. Drop dough onto fruit mixture to form 9 mounds. Bake 45 minutes or until filling is bubbly and crust is browned.

PER SERVING: Calories 240; fat 6g; chol. 0mg; prot. 3g; carbs. 49g; fiber 3g; sodium 190mg

the best of relish cookbook

date nut tart

Have some low-fat frozen yogurt on hand to top off this sweet, irresistible dessert that's perfect for the holidays. SERVES 12

1 unbaked 9-inch pastry shell

1½ cups coarsely chopped walnuts

1 cup dates, pitted and chopped (Don't use sweetened chopped dates; chop whole unsweetened dates for best results.)

⅔ cup dark corn syrup

½ cup sugar

1 teaspoon vanilla extract

½ teaspoon salt

2 large eggs, room temperature

1. Preheat oven to 350F.

2. Place pie crust in a 9-inch tart pan or roll on a lightly floured surface to fit a 13 x 3-inch pan. Press dough into sides of pan.

3. Arrange nuts and dates over dough. Combine remaining ingredients in a large bowl; whisk until well blended. Pour mixture carefully over dates.

4. Bake 50 minutes or until puffed and browned. Cool in pan on wire rack at least 15 minutes before serving.

PER SERVING: Calories 270; fat 14g; chol. 35mg; prot. 4g; carbs. 38g; fiber 2g; sodium 200mg

orange meringue pie

A seasonal spin on this classic pie, perfect with a strong cup of tea. **SERVES 8**

2 cups graham cracker crumbs

¼ cup melted butter

Cooking spray

3 eggs, separated, room temperature

1 teaspoon vanilla extract, divided

½ teaspoon salt, divided

2½ cups fresh Satsuma, tangerine or orange juice, divided

¾ cup granulated sugar

¼ cup cornstarch

¼ cup finely grated tangerine or orange rind

¼ teaspoon cream of tartar

6 tablespoons powdered sugar

1. Preheat oven to 350F.

2. Combine cracker crumbs and butter; toss with a fork until moist. Press into bottom of a 9-inch pie pan coated with cooking spray. Bake 10 minutes; cool.

3. Increase oven temperature to 375F.

4. Whisk egg yolks, ½ teaspoon vanilla, ¼ teaspoon salt and ½ cup juice in a medium bowl until smooth.

5. Combine 2 cups juice, granulated sugar, cornstarch and rind in a medium saucepan; whisk in egg yolk mixture. Cook over medium heat, whisking constantly, until thick and bubbling, about 5 minutes. Pour into crust.

6. Beat egg whites, cream of tartar, and ¼ teaspoon salt in a large bowl with a mixer at high speed until foamy, about 1 minute. Beat in powdered sugar 1 tablespoon at a time; continue beating until soft peaks form. Beat in ½ teaspoon vanilla.

7. Spread meringue over warm pie, sealing to crust's edges.

8. Bake about 15 minutes, until lightly browned and set. Cool to room temperature on a wire rack before serving.

PER SERVING: Calories 290; fat 10; chol. 95mg; prot. 4g; carbs. 47g; fiber 1g; sodium 340mg

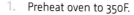

remove eggs from refrigerator *a half hour before using. Eggs at room temperature beat up to a higher volume.*

pear streusel pie

Juicy pears, fresh ginger and a cornmeal streusel topping make this pie memorable and easy.

SERVES 8

1 unbaked 9-inch pastry shell

CORNMEAL CRUMBLE:

½ cup all-purpose flour

3 tablespoons cornmeal

⅓ cup granulated sugar

¼ cup packed light brown sugar

**¼ cup unsalted butter,
cut into small pieces**

PEAR FILLING:

**7 cups firm, thinly sliced peeled
pears (about 2 pounds)**

⅔ cup granulated sugar

3 tablespoons cornstarch

1 tablespoon lemon juice

1½ teaspoons grated fresh ginger

1. Preheat oven to 425F.

2. Bake pastry shell 10 minutes; remove from oven. Cool on wire rack.

3. To prepare cornmeal crumble, combine flour, cornmeal and sugars in a large bowl. Cut in butter with a pastry blender or 2 knives until large crumbs form.

4. To prepare filling, combine all filling ingredients in a bowl; stir. Spoon into cooled pastry shell; top with crumble. Bake 15 minutes. Reduce oven temperature to 350F; bake an additional 35 minutes or until crumbs are golden brown. Cool in pan on wire rack.

PER SERVING: Calories 320; fat 11g; chol. 15mg; prot. 2g; carbs. 60g; fiber 4g; sodium 105mg

crusty rhubarb pie

Got fresh rhubarb? Here's an easy pie with a no-roll crust and a crunchy streusel topping. **SERVES 10**

PASTRY:

1½ cups all-purpose flour

1 tablespoon sugar

1 teaspoon salt

½ cup vegetable oil

2 tablespoons 2% reduced-fat milk

Cooking spray

FILLING:

**6 cups diced rhubarb
(about 3 pounds)**

2 cups sugar

6 tablespoons all-purpose flour

**1 tablespoon cold butter,
cut into small pieces**

TOPPING:

**¼ cup cold butter, cut
into small pieces**

¼ cup sugar

½ cup all-purpose flour

1. Preheat oven to 350F.

2. To prepare pastry, combine flour, sugar and salt in a medium bowl. Add vegetable oil and milk; stir well with a fork. Place dough into a deep-dish pie plate coated with cooking spray. Press pastry into bottom and up sides of pan.

3. To prepare filling, combine rhubarb, sugar and flour in a medium bowl. Spoon mixture into crust; dot with butter.

4. To prepare topping, mix butter, sugar and flour with a pastry blender or finger tips until crumbly. Sprinkle over rhubarb mixture.

5. Bake 1 hour or until filling is bubbly and topping is browned.

PER SERVING: Calories 370; fat 17g; chol. 15mg; prot. 4g; carbs. 58g; fiber 2g; sodium 270mg

the best of relish cookbook

chocolate cake with peanut butter frosting

Deep, dark, rich chocolate covered with sweet, creamy, peanut butter topping—this will bring out the kid in everyone. SERVES 20

CAKE:

Cooking spray

2 cups all-purpose flour

¾ cup granulated sugar

¾ cup packed brown sugar

⅔ cup unsweetened cocoa

1½ teaspoons baking powder

1½ teaspoons baking soda

1 teaspoon salt

2 eggs

1 cup buttermilk

½ cup vegetable oil

2 teaspoons vanilla extract

1 cup boiling water

FROSTING:

5 tablespoons butter, softened

1½ cups, plus 2 tablespoons, powdered sugar

1 teaspoon vanilla extract

1 cup smooth peanut butter

2 to 5 tablespoons 2% reduced-fat milk

1. Preheat oven to 350F. Coat a 13 x 9-inch baking pan with cooking spray.

2. To prepare cake, combine flour and next 6 ingredients (flour through salt) in a large bowl. Add eggs, buttermilk, oil and vanilla; beat vigorously with a whisk until smooth. Stir in boiling water; pour into prepared pan. Bake 35 minutes or until wooden pick inserted in the center comes out clean. Cool in pan on wire rack.

3. To prepare frosting, place butter, powdered sugar and vanilla in a medium bowl; beat with a mixer on medium speed to combine. Add peanut butter; beat until smooth. Gradually add 2 tablespoons milk, beating until very creamy. Add up to 3 additional tablespoons milk if necessary to achieve desired consistency. Spread icing over cooled cake.

PER SERVING: Calories 300; fat 16g; chol. 30mg; prot. 6g; carbs. 36g; fiber 2g; sodium 350mg

flourless chocolate cake with strawberries and cream

The addition of ground almonds provides a unique taste and texture to this rich, dense, flourless cake. **SERVES 12**

Cooking spray

2 tablespoons unsweetened cocoa

½ cup unsalted butter

1 cup, plus 2 tablespoons, sugar, divided

1 cup ground almonds

8 ounces semisweet chocolate, melted

4 eggs, separated

1 cup whipping cream

1 teaspoon vanilla extract

2 cups whole strawberries

1. Preheat oven to 350F. Coat a 9-inch springform pan with cooking spray and cocoa; shake off excess cocoa.

2. Place butter in large bowl; beat until smooth. Add 1 cup sugar; beat until creamy. Add almonds, chocolate and egg yolks; beat thoroughly with a mixer at medium speed. Set aside.

3. Beat egg whites with a mixer at high speed until soft peaks form (do not over beat). Stir one-third of egg whites into chocolate mixture; gently fold in remaining egg whites.

4. Scrape batter into prepared pan. Bake 35 to 40 minutes or until a wooden pick inserted in center comes out almost clean. Cool 30 minutes in pan on wire rack. Release sides of pan and slide onto a serving plate.

5. Combine cream, vanilla and 2 tablespoons sugar; beat until soft peaks form. Top cake with whipping cream and strawberries.

PER SERVING: Calories 330; fat 24g; chol. 45mg; prot. 4g; carbs. 30g; fiber 3g; sodium 10mg

coconut crumb cake

We love quick and easy desserts but aren't fond of cake mixes. So here's a shortcut that uses a box of vanilla wafers as the base for a cake. Dense and sweet, it's also great for breakfast or for placing in lunch boxes. **SERVES 20**

1 (12-ounce) box vanilla wafers

1 (7-ounce) can flaked sweetened coconut

2 cups sugar

1 cup chopped pecans

6 eggs

1 cup butter, melted

½ cup 2% reduced-fat milk

1. Preheat oven to 325F. Grease and flour a 12-cup bundt pan.

2. Place vanilla wafers in a food processor; pulse to form fine crumbs. Combine crumbs, coconut, sugar and pecans in a large bowl; stir to combine.

3. Place eggs, butter and milk in a medium bowl; beat with a whisk until well blended.

4. Pour egg mixture into crumb mixture; stir to mix well. (Batter will be thick.) Pour batter into prepared pan. Bake 1 hour and 35 minutes or until wooden pick inserted in center comes out clean. Cool 10 minutes in pan on wire rack; remove from pan. Cool completely on wire rack.

PER SERVING: Calories 310; fat 21g; chol. 90mg; prot. 3g; carbs. 32g; fiber 2g; sodium 80mg

honey cheesecake

Prevent the cheesecake from cracking by running a knife between the crust and pan a few minutes after removing it from the oven. The cheesecake will cool and condense without sticking to the pan's sides. SERVES 10

2 tablespoons butter, melted

⅓ cup finely ground walnuts

¼ cup vanilla wafer crumbs (5 to 6 cookies)

3 (8-ounce) blocks cream cheese, softened

¾ cup plus 2 tablespoons honey, divided

3 eggs, room temperature

¼ cup heavy cream

2 teaspoons vanilla extract

1 tablespoon all-purpose flour

½ teaspoon ground cinnamon

¼ teaspoon salt

Berries (optional)

1. Preheat oven to 325F.

2. Brush an 8- or 9-inch springform pan with melted butter. Mix walnuts and cookie crumbs in a small bowl; sprinkle evenly into pan, coating bottom and sides.

3. Beat cream cheese and ¾ cup honey with a mixer at medium speed until smooth, about 3 minutes. Scrape down sides of bowl.

4. Add eggs, one at a time; beating well after each addition. Add cream and vanilla; beat well. Add remaining ingredients; beat well. Pour batter into crust.

5. Bake 1 hour and 10 minutes or until cheesecake center barely moves when pan is touched. Remove cheesecake from oven; place on a wire rack, run a knife around outside edge. Cool to room temperature. Cover and chill at least 8 hours. When ready to serve, drizzle with remaining 2 tablespoons honey and garnish with berries, if desired.

PER SERVING: Calories 460; fat 33g; chol. 160mg; prot. 8g; carbs. 35g; fiber 0g; sodium 320mg

pumpkin cupcakes with maple cream cheese icing

Adding pumpkin to cupcakes not only adds tons of flavor, but moisture as well—without extra fat. For even more flavor, toast the walnuts before adding them to the batter. YIELD: 24 CUPCAKES

CUPCAKES:

2¼ cups all-purpose flour

1 tablespoon baking powder

½ teaspoon baking soda

½ teaspoon salt

1 teaspoon ground cinnamon

½ cup butter, softened

1⅓ cups packed brown sugar

2 eggs

1 cup canned pumpkin

¾ cup 2% reduced-fat milk

¾ cup chopped walnuts or pecans

MAPLE CREAM CHEESE ICING:

¼ cup butter, softened

1 (8-ounce) block cream cheese, softened

3 cups powdered sugar

½ cup maple syrup

2 teaspoons vanilla extract

1.   Preheat oven to 375F. Place 24 paper muffin cup liners in muffin cups.

2.   To prepare cupcakes, sift together flour and next 4 ingredients (flour through cinnamon). Place butter and sugar in a large bowl; beat with a mixer at medium speed until light and fluffy. Add eggs, 1 at a time, beating well after each addition. Add pumpkin, beating on low speed. Add flour mixture and milk alternately to sugar mixture, beginning and ending with flour, beating on low speed. Stir in nuts.

3.   Spoon batter into 24 muffin cups, filling each about two-thirds full. Bake 25 minutes or until a wooden pick inserted in center comes out clean. Cool 10 minutes in pan on wire rack; remove from pan. Cool completely on wire rack.

4.   To prepare icing, place all ingredients in large mixing bowl; beat with mixer on medium speed until smooth. Spread icing onto top of cooled cupcakes.

PER SERVING: Calories 280; fat 12g; chol. 45mg; prot. 3g; carbs. 41g; fiber 1g; sodium 220mg

chocolate relish bars

YIELD: 36 BARS

Cooking spray

1 cup all-purpose flour

1 cup whole wheat flour

2½ cups quick-cooking oats

½ teaspoon salt

1 cup packed light brown sugar

1 cup butter, softened and cut into small pieces

1½ cups raspberry jam

1 (12-ounce) package semisweet chocolate chips

1 cup chopped pecans

1. Preheat oven to 350F. Coat a 13 x 9-inch baking pan with cooking spray; line bottom and two sides with foil, letting edges extend over sides of pan. Coat foil with cooking spray; set aside.

2. Combine flours and next 3 ingredients (all-purpose flour through sugar). Add butter; combine until large crumbs form. Reserve one-third of crumb mixture.

3. Press remaining crumbs on bottom of pan. Spread jam almost to edges of crust. Sprinkle chocolate chips, reserved crumb mixture and pecans on top.

4. Bake 30 minutes, or until golden brown, covering with foil for the last 10 minutes. Cool completely on wire rack. Pull up on foil ends to remove from pan; cut into bars.

PER SERVING: Calories 210; fat 11g; chol. 15mg; prot. 2g; carbs. 30g; fiber 2g; sodium 70mg

thyme angel food cake

Serve this thyme-enhanced angel food cake with homemade ice cream you've made with the reserved egg yolks.   SERVES 12

1 cup cake flour

½ cup powdered sugar

10 egg whites, room temperature

1 teaspoon cream of tartar

½ teaspoon salt

3 tablespoons lemon juice

1 cup granulated sugar

3 tablespoons stemmed thyme leaves

2 tablespoons finely grated lemon rind

1. Preheat oven to 350F.

2. Sift flour and powdered sugar into a medium bowl; set aside.

3. Place egg whites in a large bowl; beat with a mixer at high speed until foamy. Add cream of tartar and salt; beat until soft peaks form. Beat in lemon juice. Add powdered sugar, 2 tablespoons at a time, beating well after each addition. Beat in thyme and lemon rind. Fold flour mixture into egg white mixture with a rubber spatula. Spoon batter into an ungreased 10-inch tube pan, spreading evenly. Break air pockets by cutting through batter with a knife.

4. Bake 35 minutes or until cake springs back when lightly touched. Invert pan; cool completely. Loosen cake from sides of pan using a narrow metal spatula. Invert cake onto plate.

PER SERVING: Calories 120; fat 0g; chol. 0mg; prot. 4g; carbs. 27g; fiber 0g; sodium 140 mg

almond butter oatmeal cookies

You can find almond butter under the MaraNatha label. YIELD: 24 COOKIES

10 tablespoons butter

½ cup almond butter

⅔ cup dark brown sugar

1¼ cups granulated sugar

2 eggs

1 teaspoon vanilla extract

1½ cups flour

1 teaspoon baking soda

1 teaspoon baking powder

¾ teaspoon salt

2½ cups quick-cooking oats

¾ cup coarsely chopped cashews

Preheat oven to 350F. Beat butter and almond butter until light. Add sugars and beat until light and fluffy. Beat in eggs and vanilla. Mix in flour, baking soda, baking powder and salt. Stir in oatmeal and cashews. Drop batter by tablespoons onto cookie sheets. Bake 10 to 15 minutes.

PER SERVING: Calories 210, fat 11g; chol. 30mg; prot. 4g; carbs. 27g; fiber 1g; sodium 240

molasses cookies

YIELD: 24 COOKIES

1½ cups all-purpose flour

1 cup sugar

1 teaspoon baking soda

½ teaspoon ground allspice

½ teaspoon ground nutmeg

½ teaspoon ground cloves

½ teaspoon kosher salt

½ cup vegetable shortening, melted and cooled

1 egg

¼ cup unsulfured molasses

¾ cup old-fashioned oats

1. Preheat oven to 375F.

2. Sift together flour, sugar, baking soda, spices and salt. Add melted, cooled shortening, egg and molasses; mix well. Stir in oats.

3. Drop dough by tablespoons onto an ungreased baking sheet. Flatten with bottom of a glass that has been dipped in sugar. Bake 8 to 10 minutes.

PER SERVING: Calories 100; fat 4.5g; chol. 10mg; prot. 1g; carbs. 16g; fiber 0g; sodium 95mg

gluten-free chocolate chip cookies

These tasty cookies are from Soul Dog Restaurant and Bakery in Poughkeepsie, N.Y. No one will know (or care) that they're gluten-free. YIELD: 24 COOKIES

1 cup canola oil

¾ cup sugar

¾ cup brown sugar

2 eggs

1 teaspoon vanilla

2⅓ cups Gluten-Free Baking Mix (see recipe below)

1 teaspoon baking soda

1 teaspoon salt

2 cups chocolate chips

1. Preheat oven to 350F. Grease a baking sheet.

2. Combine oil and sugar in a large bowl; beat with a mixer on medium-high speed. Add eggs, one at a time, mixing until creamy. Add vanilla.

3. Reduce speed to low and gradually add baking mix, baking soda and salt. Stir in chocolate chips.

4. Drop by level tablespoons or small ice cream scoop 2 inches apart onto baking sheet. Flatten slightly.

5. Bake 10 to 12 minutes. Remove cookies from pan; cool on wire racks.

PER SERVING: Calories 250; fat 15g; chol. 20mg; prot. 3g; carbs. 29g; fiber 2g; sodium 250mg

gluten-free baking mix

2⅓ cups chickpea flour

⅔ cup cornstarch

¼ cup sugar

3½ teaspoons xanthan gum

1½ teaspoons salt

1 teaspoon cream of tartar

Soul Dog substitutes this mix cup for cup for wheat flour, except in bread recipes. Look for xanthan gum next to the specialty flours.

Combine all ingredients. Store in an airtight container.

two cranberry ice cream

Tangy and refreshing, this buttermilk-based ice cream is a perfect ending to the richest of meals. The simple base is uncooked, or Philadelphia-style. Simply swirl in the cranberries after churning. SERVES 8

1 cup fresh cranberries

½ cup, plus 3 tablespoons, sugar, divided

⅓ cup dried cranberries

1⅓ cup heavy cream, chilled

2 cups buttermilk, chilled

2 teaspoons vanilla extract

Dash of salt

1. Place fresh cranberries and 3 tablespoons sugar in a food processor; pulse until finely chopped, pausing to scrape down sides. Stir in dried cranberries; refrigerate.

2. Combine cream, buttermilk, ½ cup sugar, vanilla and salt in a large bowl; beat well with a whisk.

3. Pour mixture into the canister of an ice-cream freezer; freeze according to manufacturer's directions.

4. When ice cream is ready, remove dasher and gently stir in cranberry mixture. Spoon ice cream into a freezer-safe container; cover and freeze at least 2 hours or until firm.

PER (½-CUP) SERVING: Calories 210; fat 16g; chol. 60mg; prot. 3g; carbs. 14g; fiber 1g; sodium 85mg

contributors

Bernstein, Michelle

Bhide, Monica

Bonom, David

Carter, Mary

Cirillo, Joan

DiResta, Dave

Disbrowe, Paula

Dragonwagon, Crescent

Eng, Christina

Feder, David

Foran, Joanne

Forberg, Cheryl

Fowler, Damon Lee

Franzo, Linda

Gold, Margo Rudman

Gold, Rozanne

Grotto, Dave

Gutierrez, Sandra

Hamaker, Brooks

Health Barn USA

Holderness, Lisa

Hosford, Doug

Hosford, Karry

Hughes, Nancy

Jachlewski, Henrietta

Jarrett, Morgan

Karadimos, Brian

Krasner, Deborah

Kressy, Jean

Maggs, Barbara

Moranville, Wini

Olmsted, Larry

Patent, Greg

Perri, Larine

Perry, Marge

Plummer, Cora Lee

Preuss, Joanna

Sanchez, Aaron

Sanders, Sharon

Scarbrough, Mark

Slemp, Theresa

Soul Dog Restaurant and Bakery

Stewart, Anne E.

Weinstein, Bruce

index